The HAPPY Beagle

Raise Your Puppy to a Happy, Well-Mannered Dog and Avoid Dog Behavior Professionals for life

- ➢ Puppy Happiness Tips
- ➢ Techniques for a Well-behaved Beagle
- ➢ Prevent Behaviour Issues
- ➢ Fulfil Your Puppy's Needs
- ➢ Be the Ideal Guardian
- ➢ Avoid Common Mistakes

Asia Moore
Dog Behavior Expert & Acclaimed Author

Copyrighted © 2019

Author: Asia Moore
www.K-9SuperHeroesDogWhispering.com
www.MustHavePublishing.com
www.KnowsToNose.com

Editor & Researcher: Alex Warrington, Ph.D.

Published by:
Worldwide Information Publishing
London
Great Britain
2019

ALL RIGHTS RESERVED. This book contains material protected under International and Federal Copyright Laws and Treaties.

Any unauthorized reprint or use of this material is strictly prohibited. No part of this book may be reproduced or transmitted in any form or by any means, electronic, mechanical or otherwise, including photocopying or recording, or by any information storage and retrieval system without express written permission from the author.

"My fashion philosophy is, if you're not covered in dog hair, your life is empty."
— Elayne Boosler

Preface

It takes time, commitment, tenacity, consistency and knowledge to raise a happy and healthy Beagle that doesn't suffer from health and behavioral issues.

This book is not like most other breed-specific books, because we believe that it's far better for all parties concerned (human and canine) to **prevent** problems rather than suffering the frustrations of living with or learning how to eliminate problems and rehabilitate a Beagle that has already developed health or behavioral issues.

It is always better to prevent unwanted behaviors than to hope you, or someone else, may have what it takes to eliminate them in the future, after your family is at their wits end, your neighbors hate you, your friends no longer visit, your dog has been deemed dangerous, and you're having guilty thoughts of re-homing every time you drive past your local SPCA.

If you want a happy, well-mannered Beagle canine companion to be a loyal, valued member of your family, it absolutely matters how you raise your dog.

Every breed has uniquely different needs. Even companion breeds, such as the Beagle, whose ancestors were originally larger dogs developed for the purpose of entertaining humans in *"bull baiting"* blood sports, that were thankfully outlawed in England over 180 years ago (1835).

For instance, a Border Collie is a very smart, high-energy dog that excels at the job of sheep herding. Therefore, if you expect this dog to sit around doing nothing all day while you're at work, you will most likely return to holes in your drywall, torn apart couches and a home that looks like it's been through a cyclone.

On the other hand, the Shih Tzu lap dog, which was originally only permitted to be owned by royalty, sat on silk pillows, was used to warm beds, has vastly different daily exercise requirements, and would be a poor choice for someone requiring a companion that could protect them from being mugged on streets ravaged by gang warfare.

Every dog breed has different talents and needs and when you decide to share your life with a particular breed, if you want a happy and well-adjusted companion, you must also be prepared to provide your dog with what he or she needs to be a happy member of your family.

Almost all canine problems, both mentally and physically, are a direct result of ignorance or unwillingness on the part of the human guardian to choose the right dog for their particular energy and lifestyle. It takes research, time and commitment to learn what each dog truly needs.

This book is uniquely different, and humans reading it need to clearly understand that the pages of this book are not all about describing what to do to eliminate problematic canine behaviors that have already occurred.

Rather, the main focus of this breed-specific book is to describe what the human guardian needs to understand and commit to doing on a daily basis in order to match the Beagle's needs, so that they can raise a happy, healthy and well-behaved dog that never has to experience behavioral issues.

Do not expect this book to be like all the others that set out endless correlations between specific mal-behaviors and what steps or actions the human guardian can take in an attempt to correct them.

In other words, this book is a totally new slant on raising a happy and healthy Beagle, because the main focus here is on the prevention of behavioral issues rather than addressing them after they have already surfaced.

About the Author

Asia Moore

Dog Behavior Expert & Acclaimed Author

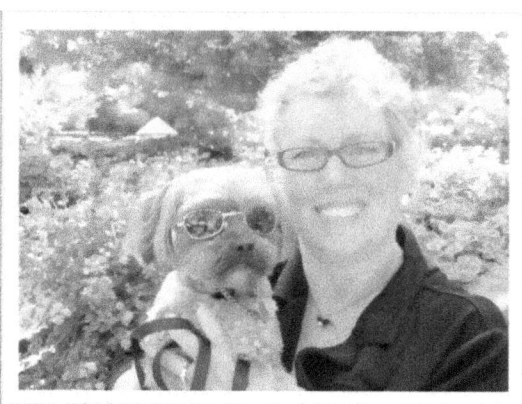

Ever since my first birthday, I was immersed in nature, and have always enjoyed a special connection with all creatures, both great and small. I learned to communicate and "talk" with many animals in their language, both wild and domesticated. At approximately the age of twelve, dogs began to become the main focus of my life, when I set about training and grooming my first puppy.

When friends and neighbors began to recognize how well behaved my dog was, and were subsequently impressed with all the tricks and routines she could perform, often without a spoken word, they asked me to train their dogs, too.

I've been so fortunate to have experienced the unconditional love of so many dogs over the years, all of who taught me many different life lessons. I began this journey with my first mixed breed ("Cindy") who protected me from my marauding brothers, then my mixed breed ("Pepper") who had an amazing human vocabulary and always knew when someone was not to be trusted, my Blue Heeler ("Bugsy") who would hike endless trails and swim miles with me, to my current loving Shih Tzu ("Boris") and all my clients' dogs in between.

Now, some 40 years later, and endless different breeds, including these patient and affectionate clowns of the dog world, and many hybrids and mutts, from tiny Chihuahuas to bouncing Belgians, a cascade of fur friends have passed through my life.

For the last 40 years, I have been managing my dog whispering, dog sitting and grooming businesses and have enjoyed countless experiences of working with dogs of all breeds and their guardians. It hasn't always been easy, and while I've had my fair share of struggles and setbacks, I've always loved and been passionate about what I do.

All these years of experience taught me invaluable lessons in all aspects of the human-canine relationship interaction. For instance, I learned how to effectively communicate with our canine friends, understand their needs and help them and their guardians lead a fulfilling and happy life together. *What could be better than that?*

Clients' dogs now remain the focal point of my dog whispering, sitting and grooming life, while I also focus on writing children's books and breed-specific books. I have so far authored over 300 books, where my goal is to pass on my knowledge and experience to all responsible dog owners (**Must Have Publishing.com**). At the same time, I continue to train human guardians, so that they can improve their relationships with their dogs and understand how to prevent and alleviate behavioral issues (**K-9 Super Heroes Dog Whispering.com**).

As well, I have recently added an additional online branch to my business, which I call "Knows To Nose" to help humans "know" how to choose the right dog "nose" for their energy and lifestyle, before they make the wrong decision and end up with troubling problems.

I am also often called upon to speak to groups about the changing roles for the canine population and how they now fit into our modern world. As well, I help humans and their chosen canines establish harmonious relationships with neighbors for those residing in multi-family living situations, such as apartment and condominium complexes.

I feel blessed that the canine world has been a major part of my life for so many years, as it never gets old. I continuously stay in touch with my clients through my business websites and personal consultations and I love how there is always room to learn more, because every unique dog brings new lessons to light and enhances everyone's life in untold, indescribable ways.

I'd like to thank you for purchasing *The Happy Beagle* and reassure you that the pages of this book contain the distilled knowledge of over 40 years experience, which, by the way, includes helping a Beagle suffering from separation anxiety.

When taken to heart, the knowledge, tips and techniques in this book can help you along your special journey inside the amazing world of our canine friends, so that you can know the unconditional love, special bond and joy that only our four-legged companions selflessly offer to us flawed humans.

Visit Asia online at the following locations:

www.K-9SuperHeroesDogWhispering.com
www.KnowsToNose.com
www.MustHavePublishing.com

Table of Contents

Chapter 1: Introduction 14

Chapter 2: Asia's Happiness Tips 18
Happy New Surroundings 19
Happy Sleep Patterns 19
Happy Puppy Play 20
Happy Puppy Housetraining 20
Happy Puppy Feeding 21
Happy Socializing 21
Happy Training 22
Happy Exercising 23
Happy Visits to the Vet 23
In a Nutshell 24

Chapter 3: Overview of the Happy Beagle 25
Vital Statistics 27
Height and Weight 27
Coat Colors and Common Features 27
How Smart is the Beagle? 28
Temperament of the Beagle 29
Happy Beagle Secrets 32
In a Nutshell 33

Chapter 4: Healthy Beagle = Happy Dog 34
Choose your veterinarian wisely 35
Consider timely neutering or spaying 35

Educate yourself with respect to vaccination 36
Be aware of the health conditions that may affect your dog 37
Educate Yourself About Common Canine Diseases and Viruses 39
Other Diseases and Viruses to Be Aware Of 40
Be aware that allergies can adversely affect your dog's health 43
Take the time to learn a little canine CPR 44
Artificial Respiration Step by Step 45
CPR Step by Step 46
In a Nutshell 47

Chapter 5: Let Your Dog BE a Happy Dog **49**
Your Beagle is Not a Child 49
In a Nutshell 52

Chapter 6: Every Happy Beagle Wants Exercise **53**
Historical Origin of the Beagle 54
Minimum Daily Exercise Requirements 55
Ideal Daily Exercise Requirements 55
In a Nutshell 60

Chapter 7: Feeding the Happy Beagle **61**
Teeth, Jaws, and Digestive Tract 62
Control of Your Happy Beagle's Food 63
Feeding Puppies 63
Feeding Adults 64
Treats 64
Dangerous Treats 65
Healthy Treats 66

The Right Food for Your Happy Beagle 67

In a Nutshell 70

Chapter 8: Care of the Happy Beagle.................... 71

Tips for Keeping Your Dog Safe.................... 72

Grooming Your Dog.................... 73

Grooming Equipment You Will Need.................... 73

Grooming Products You Will Need 74

Oops, My Dog Has Fleas.................... 75

Nail Care.................... 75

Ear Care.................... 76

Teeth Care 77

Paw Care.................... 78

In a Nutshell 78

Chapter 9: Are YOU the Ideal Happy Beagle Guardian?.................... 79

Is Your Happy Puppy Healthy?.................... 83

The Ideal Guardian 84

In a Nutshell 86

Chapter 10: Humans Make a LOT of Stupid Mistakes 87

Preventing Socialization Behavioral Issues.................... 88

Socializing With Unknown Dogs 89

Socializing With Unknown People.................... 90

Environmental Socialization.................... 90

Fear of Loud Noises 91

Accidental Rewards 93

Aggression Rewards.................... 93

Excitement Rewards 94

Interaction Rewards 95

Important Basic Rules and Boundaries 96

Adolescent Craziness 97

Less Obvious Stupid Human Mistakes 99

Flat Collar Nightmares 102

The Martingale Collar 103

Flexi-Leash Fiasco 104

In a Nutshell 107

Chapter 11: Happy Beagle Body Language 108

What's With All the Wagging and Barking? 109

What Does the Wag Mean? 109

What Does the Bark Mean? 110

In a Nutshell 115

Chapter 12: Training Basics for a Happy Beagle 117

Beagle Puppy Training Basics 119

Hand Signals 123

Simple Tricks 124

Adult Training 126

Over-Exercising 127

Playtime 127

In a Nutshell 127

Chapter 13: What If You Slip Up? 129

Chewing Inappropriate Items 131

Being Fearful of Loud Noises 131

Excessive Excitement When Friends Visit 132
Acting Aggressively on a Walk 132
Pulling When on Leash 132
Stealing Food or Raiding the Garbage Can 133
Not Obeying Commands 133
In a Nutshell 134

Chapter 14: Surprise Bonus Chapter 135

Chapter 15: Conclusion and Reviews 145

What Past Clients Have to Say 146

Chapter 1: Introduction

"Dogs are small rays of light caught on the Earth a short time to brighten our days."
— Unknown

The purpose of this book is to focus on the important steps the humans in this relationship really need to be aware of and commit to providing in order to ensure that their Beagle can live a happy and healthy life, which in turn will ensure a happy relationship for everyone.

Even though humans and dogs have been relying on one another for more than 30,000 years, it's still highly important that you take an honest look at your life, and choose the companion that is best suited to your particular lifestyle.

Within the pages of this book you will find information to help you choose wisely by providing you with a clear understanding concerning whether or not YOU have what it takes to be the right match for raising a happy and well-mannered Beagle.

In addition, this book describes in detail what the human guardian needs to keep in mind and commit to doing on a daily basis in order to match

Chapter 1: Introduction

the Beagle's needs, so that they can raise a happy, healthy and well-behaved dog that never has to experience behavioral issues.

All the information, suggestions, tips and advice given in this publication is the result of more than 40 years experience helping humans positively and effectively interact with the canine world.

If you take all that is written on these pages to heart, and regularly and consistently apply them, your Beagle will be a happy family member that will not have to suffer from any behavioral problems. In other words, the focus is placed on prevention, rather than trying to correct any issues after they have surfaced.

Every Chapter of this book contains valuable information that will provide you with a solid understanding of the breed and the steps you need to take to raise a happy and well-behaved Beagle.

For instance, **Chapter 2** – *"Asia's Happiness Tips"* sets out a summary of what she personally believes makes for a happy Beagle and encourages you to ask yourself what YOU think would make this dog happy.

Chapter 3 – *"Overview of the Happy Beagle"* will outline vital statistics, coat colors and common features, intelligence, temperament and interesting secrets and facts that may not be commonly known. In order to raise a contented Beagle, you need to have some basic knowledge of the breed to help you choose wisely so that you are able to comprehend their needs.

Chapter 4 – *"Healthy Beagle = Happy Dog"* is where you will find out what you need to know about medical care, safety and health issues that may affect the Beagle breed, including common diseases and viruses, allergies and canine CPR procedures that could save a life. Needless to say, if your Beagle is not physically healthy, he or she will not be a happy canine companion for very long, because suffering from health-related issues will undoubtedly create a miserable and ill-mannered dog.

In **Chapter 5** – *"Let Your Dog BE a Happy Dog"*, you will find information about how to let your Beagle actually BE a dog, rather than

Chapter 1: Introduction

attempting to turn them into a fur human, which can make for a very confused, unhappy and ill-mannered canine.

Chapter 6 – *"Every Happy Beagle Wants Exercise"*, first outlines some of the original history of this breed; if you know what they were bred to do, you will better understand how important it is to commit to the daily exercise routines recommended in this book, without which the Beagle will not be happy for very long.

Chapter 7 – *"Feeding the Happy Beagle"*, is where you will find information about the structure of the canine jaw, various food options and feeding suggestions as well as treats to avoid for raising a happy and healthy companion.

In **Chapter 8** – *"Care of the Happy Beagle"*, you will find travel safety tips, licensing, insurance, grooming procedures and important care of nails, ears, teeth and paws, all of which will help you to raise a happy Beagle. While this information might seem generic, imagine how you might feel going for months without washing your hair, cutting your nails or brushing your teeth. Unfortunately, that is the reality for many dogs, because their owners have not been properly advised with respect to the importance of good grooming habits. How happy and well behaved do you think such an ill-cared for Beagle would be?

Chapter 9 – *"Are YOU the Ideal Happy Beagle Guardian?"* is concerned with asking yourself some serious questions, including whether your energy, activity, commitment and lifestyle matches that of what the Beagle needs to be happy and well behaved. It's vital for you to give serious consideration to these questions when considering the Beagle breed, because should you choose the wrong dog to share your life with, everybody will be miserable.

Chapter 10 – *"Humans Make a LOT of Stupid Mistakes"* outlines that far too often we humans, without even realizing it, are the cause of creating behavioral problems in our canine companions. You will find out what are some of the common mistakes to avoid (and the right thing to do!) when it comes to socialization, accidental rewards, fear of noises, the right collars, basic rules and boundaries, adolescent craziness and more. Simply being aware of the many mistakes we

Chapter 1: Introduction

humans can often inadvertently be guilty of when raising our canine companions, can mean the difference between a Happy Beagle with no behavioral issues or a life of frustration and correction.

Chapter 11 – *"Happy Beagle Body Language"*, outlines the basics of learning canine body language, and will help you be safe around other dogs. Learning to properly "read" a dog's intentions can prevent an unwanted encounter with another canine or human, and this will help to ensure that everyone remains happy.

In Chapter 12 – *"Training Basics for a Happy Beagle"*, you will learn valuable training tips and routines that will help to keep your dog truly happy and well behaved for their entire life. It's no surprise that a properly trained Beagle will be a much happier companion that everyone enjoys being around, and will be far less likely to develop behaviour issues later in life. Developing a basic training program and learning to teach your dog commands and discipline is all part of starting your dog off on the right paw.

Chapter 13 – *"What If You Slip Up?"* is only necessary because we humans tend to get too busy and overwhelmed with the rigors of daily living, which means we sometimes forget to be consistent with providing what our Beagle may need to be happy. If you slip up, this Chapter has outlined a few of the more common behavioral issues and how to quickly get yourself back on track.

Chapter 14 – *"Surprise Bonus Chapter"* is a Question and Answer section containing a few human/canine situations, with humans asking questions and wise words from the perspective of the affectionate and often comical Beagle, as the dog answers the questions.

Take heed humans, because when you honestly assess your own compatibility, lifestyle and energy level for being the right guardian for the Beagle, and are vigilant about following the advice and tips outlined in the following pages, you can raise a healthy and happy dog that will be a joy to live with and will never have to suffer from any behavioral issues.

Chapter 2: Asia's Happiness Tips

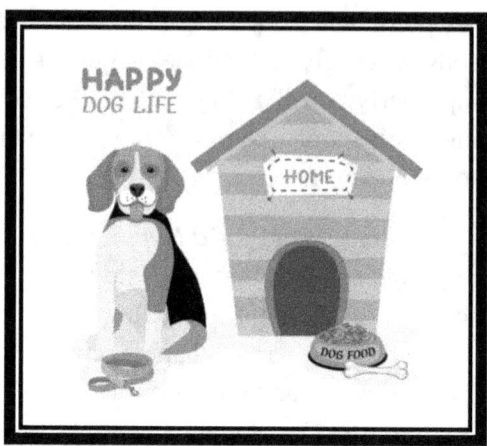

"There is no psychiatrist in the world like a puppy licking your face."
— Ben Williams

The following few paragraphs are a summary of my own personal ramblings, beliefs, and ideas about what I think makes for a happy Beagle.

While I hope you may wholeheartedly agree, it's absolutely okay if you have other ideas, or if you may have an entirely different take on this subject, because we will all have our own "personal" ideas about what constitutes happiness for a Beagle, and if your ideas are different from mine, this does not mean that they are any less valid.

If you're considering sharing your life with a Beagle, and have never before really sat down and consciously thought about what would make this particular breed truly happy, while you may gain a little insight from reading about my own personal beliefs, I encourage you to take the time to do this exercise yourself. If you have a family, get them involved in this fun exercise, too.

When you take the time to sit with a piece of paper and pen and begin to write down what YOU think makes a Beagle happy, you may be

Chapter 2: Asia's Happiness Tips

surprised about what surfaces, and this simple exercise may inspire you and your family to discover new ways to bond with your dog, which will be the basis of having a truly happy relationship.

I'll help to get you started with the following question:
"What do you think would make a Beagle happy?"

I believe that the very best start you can make, with respect to "happiness" when first bringing home your new Beagle puppy is to do all you can to reassure him or her that they are not alone (see below).

Happy New Surroundings

The puppy will be understandably nervous about the new and unfamiliar faces, surroundings and smells, and will be missing their mother, other siblings and everything in their environment they had grown used to during their first 8 to 10 weeks of life.

Make sure that you don't overwhelm your new puppy with too much all at once. For instance, close off rooms that you don't need access to and encourage your puppy to come to you as you wander about in a smaller space.

Happy Sleep Patterns

When it's time to go to bed, take your puppy outside for a bathroom break, and then make sure that you have a nice, cozy kennel all ready for your new puppy with a soft lining or blanket and place their new bedroom inside your room, so that they will be able to hear and see you.

Unless you want your Beagle to sleep on your bed when they're fully grown, now is the time to exercise a little tough love as the new puppy will most likely not want to be alone in their kennel and will prefer sleeping next to you.

If your bed is large enough to accommodate their kennel, this is the best way to help your puppy have a happy sleep time because they will be next to you, but still inside their own kennel, and as they grow larger they will be used to their kennel and will not mind that it is sitting on the floor. Congratulations! You've just created a routine that will ensure happy sleeping patterns for your dog.

Happy Puppy Play

Taking the time for regular play sessions with your new Beagle puppy will certainly make them very happy, so make sure you set aside several times during your day when you stop with the human work and chores and engage your puppy in fun games for 10 or 15 minutes at least three or four times a day.

Every puppy and dog needs some time in their day where they can relax and play a fun game, and this is the beginning of trust and respect between you and your fur friend.

Happy Puppy Housetraining

One of the very first things your new Beagle puppy needs to learn is where the bathroom is, and the more vigilant you are, the fewer "accidents" will occur, which will make both of you much happier.

Learn to pay attention and understand your dog's body language, so that you can help teach them proper bathroom habits at a very young age. This is a very smart dog and it should not be difficult to quickly train them that outside is their bathroom.

When they wake up, take them outside immediately. Twenty minutes after they have eaten a meal, take them outside to relieve themselves. After a play session or when they've had a big drink of water, take them outside. After they've gone pee or number 2, immediately praise and reward them with a treat.

Yes, to do this right, you and your puppy will be spending a lot of time going outside, but once their bladder grows larger and stronger, the number of hours he or she can "hold" it will increase, and the number of times your dog will have to visit the great outdoor bathroom during each day will markedly decrease.

Use this bathroom training time also as a way to create a strong bond between you and your dog and as their first lessons in leash training and reward training for doing what you ask; if you take the time to go out with them while they're on leash, it's easy to train your dog to "go" on command, and as they mature, you'll be very glad that you took the time to do this.

Happy Puppy Feeding

It's not rocket science to understand that providing your puppy or dog with the best nutrition from the very first day you bring them home will lead to a healthy fur friend, which in turn, will lead to a feel-good, energetic and happy companion.

Be aware of the importance of what you feed your dog and commit to doing the best you can to keep your canine friend healthy and happy. Read labels and feed them only the highest-quality food, so they have the best opportunity for a long life.

While it's important to start your puppy off with the right food, it's just as important to continue to feed your adult dog the very best diet. Please refer to Chapter 7 (Feeding the Happy Beagle), where you will read about types of food, appropriate treats and more.

Happy Socializing

Socializing a new puppy is one of the most important steps you can take to ensure that your chosen companion lives a happy and stress-free life.

When you don't take the time to properly socialize your Beagle puppy, and indeed, keep on socializing throughout their lifetime, you can create many behavioral issues, some of which can be so severe that your dog may be in danger of having their life prematurely shortened, should they act out aggressively toward a human or other animal.

Many times, I've been called upon to help a human alleviate aggressive tendencies being displayed by their canine companion, and in pretty much every instance, this could have been entirely avoided if the dog had been properly trained and socialized.

Every dog must have a leader, and sturdy, often stubborn or independent-minded dogs that have a history of being bred for hunting, such as the Beagle, when not properly socialized, trained and taught to respect the word of their human guardians will be forced to take over the family "pack" and make human decisions. Unfortunately, this can get them and you into all sorts of unwanted troubles, should they decide to act out in an aggressive manner.

Any sort of aggression is a huge stress on both dog and human and, as we are all aware, stress shortens lives and prevents anyone from experiencing happiness, so help make your dog happy and make sure that you don't place the very heavy burden of making human decisions on the shoulders of your canine companion..

While early socialization of a puppy is very important, keep in mind that it's just as important to continue your adult dog's socialization throughout their lifetime. Please refer to Chapter 10 (Humans Make a LOT of Stupid Mistakes), that outlines the many aspects of socializing your Beagle.

Happy Training

Almost as important as proper socializing to keep your dog happy, is proper training, which should never be overlooked, unless you want to create an unstable Beagle that thinks they are the boss of all they survey.

This friendly, high-energy breed can be surprisingly versatile and able to excel at almost anything you have the time to teach and in order to keep this dog happy and they need to have both their body regularly exercised and their brain regularly challenged. Keep in mind that as a result of this hound dog's very strong sense of smell, they can tend to be very single minded when they catch a scent, which means much patience will be required during training.

Start training this dog as soon as you bring him or her home from the breeder and you will have given yourself the best opportunity to have a happy, eager to comply and safe companion at your side before they are six months old. Of course, you will start out with very short training sessions of no more than a few minutes at a time, and as they slowly mature, you can increase the length of your sessions.

Chapter 2: Asia's Happiness Tips

Make sure any training is a fun and happy time for both you and your dog, with lots of happy praise and treats, and he or she will quickly learn to trust and respect you as their leader and be eager for their next session.

While this puppy can begin training at an early age, when you continue their training throughout their life, this energetic companion will usually be an eager participant that is entirely capable of learning several canine sports. See more in Chapter 12 (Training Basics for a Happy Beagle).

Happy Exercising

While the Beagle can excel with training and learning new routines, which is exercise as well, they also need some down time, or some time off from your vigilant supervision.

Just like us humans, who need time where they don't have to think about work, our dogs also need some free time where they can enjoy romping and playing with the family or exploring the local woodland paths, rolling in the grass or lazing in the warm sunshine, and just being a dog.

The Beagle,is an active dog with great stamina, which means that he or she will require a moderate to high amount of minimal daily exercise requirements, to keep them mentally healthy and physically fit. You can learn much more about the exercises that will keep this dog happy in Chapter 6 (Every Happy Beagle Wants Exercise).

Happy Visits to the Vet

Even though you may be feeding the best food, properly exercising, and training your dog to be a calm and obedient member of your family, you will also want to have at least yearly visits to your chosen veterinarian's office to make sure all is well.

Start taking your dog to the vet's office even when they don't have any reason to be there, other than to receive a treat and friendly greetings, so that they get used to the different smells and people who work there because when you do this, your dog will learn that visits to the vet's office can be a happy time.

While it's ideal to get your puppy used to visits to the vet's office when they are still young, there is much you can do throughout the life of your adult dog that will help to keep these visits to a minimum. Be sure to read Chapter 8 (Care of the Happy Beagle) that outlines many things you can do to help ensure your dog remains as healthy as possible.

Back to the pen and paper exercise.

When you pay attention, and take the time to think about the many things you can do that will keep your dog happy, even more ideas will present themselves along the way, and you and your chosen canine companion will enjoy a long and happy life together. Take my word for it, *do take the exercise* and you will thank me later.

In a Nutshell

The above paragraphs are a short synopsis of what I think makes for a Happy Beagle, and I'm sure you may have many more ideas to contribute to this list.

The following Chapters of this book contain much more detail concerning what every conscientious Beagle guardian needs to commit to, on a daily basis, in order to ensure that the human family and the Happy Beagle have the best opportunity for living a long, happy and healthy life together without ever having to experience any unwanted behavioral issues.

When you want to raise a Happy Beagle that is a joy to share your life with, you will want to carefully read through all the coming Chapters, while always keeping in mind, not just what makes you and your family happy, but what makes your dog happy as well.

Chapter 3: Overview of the Happy Beagle

*"Once you have a wonderful dog,
a life without one is a life diminished."*
— Dean Koontz

I cannot stress enough how important it is that you understand the basics of any breed, such as size, energy level, intelligence, temperament, and exercise requirements, so that you can truly understand if you are the right person or family for sharing your life with a particular dog.

In order to raise a happy Beagle you need to gain some basic knowledge, because this will help you choose wisely to ensure that your lifestyle and daily routine can meet this dog's needs.

For instance, you need to know that the muscular, yet gentle Beagle is a purebred scent hound that has superior tracking skills, and is a member of the Hound Dog category. In the past, this dog was primarily developed for hunting hare. Today, and when not simply a family pet, this breed is primarily employed as a detection dog for quarantined foodstuffs and prohibited drugs or other agricultural products (as a result of their superior sense of smell). In other words, this is NOT a dog that will be happy spending many hours alone watching the grass grow while you're away at work.

Chapter 3: Overview of the Happy Beagle

The friendly Beagle is an intelligent, even-tempered dog that can easily become distracted by their very sensitive nose, because next to the Bloodhound, the Beagle has one of the most highly developed senses of smell, especially when searching along the ground. This often means that they may be difficult to control when they have caught an interesting scent.

Interestingly, the Beagle is more popular in Canada and the United States than in their native Great Britain, and as a result of their gentle dispositions, are often seen as a favorite family pet.

Perhaps the most endearing feature of the Beagle is their large, dark, pleading eyes that could melt the heart of the most stoic. This is also a reason why many of these dogs end up being overweight, as humans have great difficulty resisting the pleading stare when there is any food involved.

This gentle, amiable and happy canine will not be an especially good guard dog, although they will bark or howl if they hear an unfamiliar sound, which makes them a good watchdog.

Although the Beagle tends to be easily excitable, they are not known to be aggressive or overly timid, either, and with consistent training and regular exercise they can learn to contain their excited energy and be well-mannered.

The Beagle is an all-round versatile dog that also has great stamina and determination, especially when engaged in any sort of hunting activity, which means that this dog can sometimes be difficult to train as they easily become distracted by smells.

One of the reasons the Beagle is such a popular family canine breed is because they are gentle with children. However, they are definitely pack oriented, which means that they can suffer from anxiety if expected to spend many lonely hours without the company and direction of their human guardian.

For instance, a Beagle left alone for many long hours may develop barking, baying or howling tendencies, and they may also bay or howl when they catch an interesting scent.

Chapter 3: Overview of the Happy Beagle

Generally speaking, while the coat color, size and temperament of the Beagle will largely depend upon the appearance and size of both breeding parents, this will be a small, short-haired hound dog with a muscular, compact body, that resembles a miniature Foxhound, with a square cut muzzle, large eyes, long ears, and a merry temperament that thrives when receiving plenty of your time and attention.

The main overview of the breed is outlined below and is the foundation of choosing a Beagle wisely and raising a happy and well-behaved dog.

Vital Statistics

While every dog is unique, there are standards that are common to each purebred canine, such as height, weight and various coat colors and features. You can also get a pretty good idea of what the puppies will look like when full grown, when you see their parents.

Height and Weight

When measured at the shoulder, the Beagle may stand between 11 and 13 inches (27.9 and 33 centimetres) and weigh between 19 and 28 pounds (8 and 12 kilograms) or more, depending on the size of both breed parents.

Coat Colors and Common Features

The Beagle has a short, smooth, close fitting coat that has a harsh feel to the touch and sheds all year round. The coat will be fairly low maintenance (except twice yearly when they may shed more heavily), and in order to keep this coat looking it's best, they will require regular brushing.

While the Beagle is often tri-colored (black, white and tan), all typical hound color combinations are acceptable in the show ring. Interestingly, because this dog is considered to be a hunting breed, should they be displayed in the show ring with any scars (from hunting), this will not be considered a fault, but rather an "honorable wound".

Eyes will be large-sized, round-shaped and brown or hazel in color with a soft, gentle and pleading expression. This dog's ears will be long, broad with rounded tips, and close the head, reaching almost to the end of the nose, and this dog carries a naturally medium-length tail (that has a white tip), gaily over the back in a slight curve.

This merry and sociable breed is known for their stamina, smaller size, compact and muscular body, large and expressive eyes, and independent determination.

How Smart is the Beagle?

While every dog is surprisingly different even within the same breed, despite what some "experts" might have to say about it, you need to keep in mind that there are *"people smarts"* and *"dog smarts"* and that these two ways of rating intelligence are often widely divergent or in conflict with one another.

If you really want to rate your Beagle's intelligence, based on what we humans think is *"smart"*, there is a book *("The Intelligence of Dogs")* written in 1994 by Stanley Coren, which has become the standard for rating the particular intelligence of different canine breeds.

While I can agree, in part, with some of the information contained in this book, I can also disagree, because of personal experience, as I have found that some dogs that are rated very low on the intelligence scale are also very smart in their own way. In the case of the Beagle's low rating on the intelligence scale, this is likely the result of their superior sense of smell, which can make them difficult to train because they lose focus when an interesting smell attracts their attention.

Therefore, I caution you not to pre-handicap your dog's level of intelligence just because of something you may have read in a well-respected book, because each dog has their own unique set of talents and much of how they develop is up to their guardian.

Coren judges canine intelligence of particular purebred canines based on three categories, as follows:

*"**Instinctive Intelligence** – a dog's ability to carry out tasks it was bred to perform, such as guarding, herding, hunting, pointing, retrieving or supplying companionship."*

Chapter 3: Overview of the Happy Beagle

*"**Adaptive Intelligence** – how well a dog is able to solve problems on its own."*

*"**Working/Obedience Intelligence** – how quickly a dog is able to learn from humans."*

In the case of the Beagle, Coren places this companion dog in the *"Lowest Degree of Working/Obedience Intelligence"* category, which means that while they may not appear to be the sharpest crayon in the box, due to their independent nature, they apparently have the ability to understand new commands after between 80 and 100 repetitions, and when properly trained, the ability to obey first commands 25% of the time, or less.

Please keep in mind that there are always exceptions to every study and a particular breed's degree of intelligence is often related to their early upbringing and how they are trained.

However, there is no doubt that with the proper training method and plenty of patience, the Beagle is still easily trainable, and they will be happy and mentally fit so long as they are permitted to spend most of their time in the company of their human guardians.

Temperament of the Beagle

A Beagle is certainly going to be an energetic, fun loving, happy dog with great stamina that lives to run and play, however, you need to keep in mind that this dog, when not trained properly at a young age, can become very vocal. Often, these dogs end up in shelters and rescue facilities because the neighbors complain about the noise when this dog is left alone.

Every dog needs the discipline of being walked on leash outside of the home each day, as well as the opportunity for off-leash time to run and play fetch or enjoy socializing with other dogs, and these dogs bond strongly to humans of all ages, and truly love everyone they meet along their exciting road of life.

Chapter 3: Overview of the Happy Beagle

Remember that this dog is a natural scent hound, which means that they could have a high prey drive, and if not well trained and given the opportunity, they may take off after an interesting scent, such as rabbits, cats or even deer.

This breed will become very attached and devoted to its family members, and they will not usually be aggressive toward strangers or other dogs, unless they have not been properly socialized at a young age.

This is an alert, intelligent, affectionate, energetic, fun-loving, clever and sometimes distracted dog that will not only enjoy plenty of exercising, this will be essential to their health. If you neglect this dog and do not provide them with regular daily exercise and mental stimulation, they will create their own entertainment, which could include destroying your property or barking and howling to excess.

The Beagle will need to be well and continually socialized at a young age, and taught to keep their boundless enthusiasm under control. They will be interested participants that enjoy being involved in all of the family's activities, especially if they involve following a scent or endless types of exercising.

Most Beagles are sturdy, yet loving, gentle and faithful companions, always ready for the next adventure, that are great for children that understand how to respect a dog and seniors who can give them all the attention they crave and the exercise they need.

The people-loving Beagle will be an active dog that is an impressive jumper, climber, and intuitive problem solver who will excel at any activity you have the time to engage in.

You will want to keep in mind that this is a highly food motivated dog, which means that portion control at dinnertime and plenty of exercise will be a necessary part of their daily life.

This dog has great stamina and needs to be able to eliminate pent up energy by exercising their minds and their bodies so that they can remain a healthy weight.

Chapter 3: Overview of the Happy Beagle

One of my clients had a Beagle that was suffering badly from separation anxiety because he left her alone all day (except for a quick trip home at lunchtime to let her out for a bathroom break), while he was as work. Understandably, the neighbors were constantly complaining about the howling. This dog had to be re-homed, and now happily enjoys life on a hobby farm with no close neighbors.

This is NOT a dog that will ever be happy spending so many hours alone, so unless you work at home, or are retired, this is NOT the dog for you.

All guardians need to be fully aware that any dog that does not receive early and continual socialization throughout their lifetime may learn to become aggressive when he or she encounters people, unknown dogs and other animals, visiting neighborhood children, friends or unfamiliar situations.

Most likely, the first thing you will want to teach your Beagle will be to keep their puppy exuberance under control, so that they do not knock over children or unstable seniors in their happiness to enthusiastically greet everyone.

The sturdy Beagle is very social and will be a good choice for families with older children, and can definitely be a good companion for older adults who have the energy, time and mobility required to provide this happy dog with the moderate to high daily exercise they need.

This dog should not be left alone or unsupervised outside, even in what you might think is a securely fenced yard. This is because in combination with street smarts and athletic abilities, they are capable of figuring out problems, which could involve putting their strong legs to use when scaling heights or climbing fencing that no other dog would ever consider attempting.

Never forget that the Beagle is a scent hound with a superior sense of smell that will encourage them to free themselves from any sort of confining situation in order to follow an interesting scent or fulfil their social need to be amongst a pack.

Bottom line, the Beagle will usually be a happy companion that is friendly and accepting of both unknown dogs and humans, but when not trained to live a calm life, they can suffer from attachment issues if expected to spend time alone.

Happy Beagle Secrets

The Beagle's officially recognized name is "Beagle", and while there is some controversy over where this name originally came from, some believe that this word came from the Celtic word for small, which is *"beag"*.

Beagle type dogs have existed for more than 2,500 years.

During the time when the sport of hunting hare was an all-day pastime, this was referred to as *"beagling"*.

The world's most famous Beagle is a 1960's cartoon character named *"Snoopy"*, from the "Peanuts" comic strip, created by Charles M. Schulz.

"Odie" is another famous Beagle cartoon character that was Garfield, the cat's sidekick, in the Jim Davis comic strip that was popular in the late 1970's.

The United States Customs and Border Patrol use Beagles in their *"Beagle Brigade"* to detect contraband agricultural products that may bring dangerous insects or diseases into the US inside airport luggage arriving from foreign countries. Every year, these super sniffers help to confiscate approximately 75,000 prohibited products.

The white tip on the end of a Beagle's tail has been purposefully bred into this breed so that they can be easily seen when their nose is following a scent on the ground and their tail is sticking straight up.

The Beagle nose has approximately 220 million scent receptors, as compared to humans who only have 5 million, or many other canine breeds who have half as many as the Beagle.

Many well known individuals have chosen to share their lives with this merry and social little hound, including the 36th President of the United

Chapter 3: Overview of the Happy Beagle

States (Lyndon B. Johnson), British Veterinary surgeon and writer, James Herriot, and American singer/songwriter, Barry Manilow.

One of *the* most popular breeds of dogs worldwide, (according to 2019 American Kennel Club registrations), the incredibly popular Beagle has consistently held a top ten popularity ranking amongst the 194 registered breeds for many years.

In a Nutshell

Familiarizing yourself with the Beagle's size, weight, early history and special attributes and what they were originally developed to do, plus understanding their intelligence level and temperament will help you to decide if this dog is the right one for you.

Obtaining a comprehensive understanding of the breed's needs will not only save you and your dog from much future grief, but it will be a prerequisite for raising a content, well-behaved, and happy dog that you are proud to call your best friend and companion.

Chapter 4: Healthy Beagle = Happy Dog

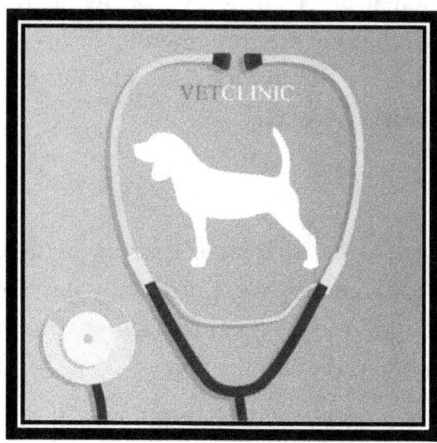

"Dogs have a way of finding the people who need them, and filling an emptiness we didn't ever know we had."
— Thom Jones

If your Beagle is not physically healthy, he or she will not be a happy canine companion for very long, because suffering from health-related issues can easily create a miserable and ill-mannered dog.

It's prudent that you take the many steps outlined here to help ensure that you are doing all that you can to keep on top of your Beagle's good health.

Make sure you take the time to choose a veterinarian that can provide yearly check-ups, have your dog spayed or neutered in a timely fashion, choose a healthy diet for him or her, and carefully read this section so that you educate yourself about issues that may adversely affect your dog's health.

As well, take the time to learn a little canine CPR, because doing so may save the life of your own dog, or someone else's.

Chapter 4: Healthy Beagle = Happy Dog

Below you will find more information on each one of these steps you need to take to raise a healthy and happy Beagle.

Choose your veterinarian wisely

Some clinics specialize in caring for smaller pets, while some specialize in larger animal care, and others have a wide-ranging area of expertise and will care for all animals, including livestock and reptiles.

Choosing a good veterinary clinic will be very similar to choosing the right health care clinic or doctor for your own personal health, because you want to ensure that your puppy or adult dog receives the quality care they deserve. A good place to begin your search will be by asking other dog owners where they take their furry friends and whether they are happy with the service they receive.

It's also a good idea to take your Beagle into your chosen clinic several times before they actually need to be there for any treatment, so that they are not fearful of the new smells and unfamiliar surroundings.

Consider timely neutering or spaying

There are varying opinions on the topic of the best time to neuter or spay your young Beagle. One thing that most veterinarians do agree on is that earlier spaying or neutering, between 4 and 6 months of age, can be a better choice than waiting longer.

Keep in mind that non-neutered or spayed males and females are more likely to display aggression related to sexual behaviour, than are dogs that have been neutered or spayed.

For instance, fighting, particularly in male dogs that is directed at other males, is less common after neutering. The intensity of other types of aggression, such as irritable aggression in females will be totally eliminated by spaying, so make that appointment at the vet's office and get it done.

Effects on General Temperament: many dog owners often become needlessly worried that a neutered or spayed dog will lose their vigor, when in fact, many unwanted, aggressive qualities, resulting from hormonal impact, may resolve after surgery, and you will be acting as a conscientious, informed, and caring guardian.

Effects on Escape and Roaming: a neutered or spayed Beagle is less likely to wander, and castrated male dogs have the tendency to patrol smaller sized outdoor areas and are less likely to participate in territorial conflicts with perceived opponents.

Possible Weight Gain: while metabolic changes that occur after spaying or neutering can cause some puppies to gain weight, often the real culprit for any weight gain is the human who feels guilty for subjecting their puppy to this medical procedure, and in an attempt to make themselves feel better, they feed more treats or meals to their companion.

If you notice weight gain after neutering or spaying your Beagle puppy, simply adjust their food and treat consumption as needed and once stitches are healed, make sure that they are receiving adequate daily exercise.

Educate yourself with respect to vaccination

It has now become common practice to vaccinate adult dogs every three years, and if your veterinarian is insisting on a yearly vaccination for your puppy, you need to ask them why, because to do otherwise is considered by many professionals to be *"over vaccinating"*.

Whether or not your dog actually needs a booster can be determined with a simple blood test at your vet's office, so be proactive, and ask for a blood test.

Puppies need to be vaccinated in order to provide them with protection against four common and serious diseases referred to as *"DAPP"*, which stands for Distemper, Adenovirus, Parainfluenza and Parvo Virus.

Approximately one week after your puppy has completed all three sets of primary DAPP vaccinations, they will be fully protected from those specific diseases.

Chapter 4: Healthy Beagle = Happy Dog

Be aware of the health conditions that may affect your dog

While a healthy, happy Beagle may live to be 12 to 15 years or more, and with healthy breeding practices and proper care may not suffer from any noted health problems, it's important to be aware of health concerns that have been known to affect this breed, such as some of the more common issues listed below:

Obesity: the Beagle is almost as well known for being prone to being overweight, as they are known for their heightened sense of smell. This is a dog that has a voracious appetite and can sniff out food a mile away. Obesity can lead to joint problems and heart disease.

Hypothyroidism: is an underactive thyroid condition in which the gland does not produce enough hormone, which can lead to a slower metabolism, which in turn can lead to weight gain, tiredness, delays in growth, and intolerance to cold. Treatment involves thyroid replacement therapy.

Dwarfism: in the Beagle can cause a condition called *"funny puppy syndrome"*, in which a puppy physically develops with a crooked back and weak legs.

Corneal Ulcers: when the clear outer capsule in the dog's eye becomes irritated, scratched or somehow damaged through injury that is left untreated, the area becomes inflamed and bacteria can enter which can then lead to infection which will then cause an ulcer.

A dog suffering from a scratch or an ulcer on the cornea of the eye will be experiencing pain, tearing and itching and often discharge and will often squint and paw at the eye, which can make the problem worse.

Treatment will depend upon how severe the ulcer may be and while milder cases will involve applying antibiotic ointments, more severe cases can involve surgery.

Glaucoma: this eye disease, which is usually caused by an increase of fluid pressure in the eye, can cause permanent damage to the dog's vision in the affected eye or eyes, which, if left untreated, can lead to blindness.

Chapter 4: Healthy Beagle = Happy Dog

Retinal Dysplasia: this eye disease appears as streaks or dots in the retina of the dog's eye, which can lead to blindness.

Cherry Eye: many breeds can suffer from this genetic eye problem, including the Beagle; the gland of the third eyelid prolapses or slips in the corner of the eye, as a result of weakness of the connective tissue surrounding the gland, causing a pink fleshy protrusion to extend or bulge over the edge of the dog's eyelid.

Although it is possible for this problem to self-correct, it is recommended to take your dog to the veterinarian as soon as you notice this condition, because treatment will require pushing the prolapsed gland back into the pocket.

Entropion: is a condition in which the dog's eyelid will roll inward, which then causes the lashes to rub against the eyeball. Left untreated, this condition can severely damage the dog's eye, even causing blindness. Surgery is required to correct this problem.

Ectropion: in a dog suffering from this condition, the lower eyelid will turn outward and requires surgery to repair.

Otitis Externa: is an inflammation of the ear canal, which can become chronic, and causes discomfort, irritation and pain. Ear infections are common to Beagles due to their long, floppy ears, which prevents the inner ear from receiving enough airflow to keep the ears dry.**Cerebellar Cortical Degeneration**: a puppy affected by this rare disease will have trouble with coordination, causing them to move slower, fall often or have an irregular gait. There is a genetic test available to rule out this type of degeneration, which affects 0.1% of dogs.

Immune Mediated Polygenic Arthritis: is another rare condition caused when the Beagle's immune system attacks the dog's joints, which can occur at a young age. Steroid treatments can sometimes be effective in alleviating symptoms..

Reverse Sneezing: more often seen in short-nosed (brachycephalic) breeds of dogs, can also affect the Beagle. A dog having a reverse sneezing episode will often make a sound that sounds like goose honking, which is a rapid drawing of air in through the nose and mouth.

This can occur for a variety of reasons, such as over-excitement, exercising in hot weather or irritants in the air causing sinus irritation. Episodes usually only last a few seconds with no apparent ill effects to the dog.

Epilepsy: most epileptic seizures can be controlled medically. However, it is very important to have a dog immediately diagnosed by a veterinarian if seizures begin, so that the severity of the condition can be properly assessed.

Chinese Beagle Syndrome: is an abnormal growth of the dog's skull that grows wider than normal and creates slanted eyes. Otherwise, the growth of the dog is normal, however, dogs with CBS often will also have abnormal toes and heart problems. There is no DNA test for this usually rare syndrome.

Educate Yourself About Common Canine Diseases and Viruses

While your dog may never suffer from a common disease or virus, in order to ensure the safety and health of your happy Beagle, you need to be aware of the many common diseases and viruses that could detrimentally affect the health of your dog.

Always watch out for the symptoms of the following common diseases and if you suspect that your dog has been infected, contact your vet immediately.

Distemper (sometimes called *"hard pad disease"*): is a contagious, serious, and deadly viral illness that is spread through the air or by direct or indirect contact with a dog (or other animal) that is already infected (such as ferrets, raccoons, foxes, skunks and wolves), that can also cause thickening of the pads on the feet or nose.

Early symptoms include fever, loss of appetite and mild eye inflammation that may only last a day or two, with symptoms becoming more serious and noticeable as the disease progresses. There is no known cure.

Adenovirus: causes infectious canine hepatitis, which can range in severity from very mild to very serious. The treatment focuses on management of symptoms, and the condition can sometimes result in death. Symptoms can vary and may include coughing, loss of appetite, increased thirst and urination, tiredness, vomiting and seizures.

Canine Parainfluenza Virus (CPIV): also referred to as *"canine influenza virus"*, *"greyhound disease"* or *"race flu"*, which is easily spread through the air or by coming into contact with respiratory secretions. While it is usually a self-limiting virus that will run its course within a couple of weeks, in severe cases and without antibiotic treatment, it may be fatal.

Symptoms can include a dry, hacking cough, difficulty breathing, wheezing, runny nose and eyes, sneezing, fever, loss of appetite, tiredness, depression and possible pneumonia. In cases where only a cough exists, tests will be required to determine whether the cause of the cough is the parainfluenza virus or the less serious *"kennel cough"*.

Canine Parvovirus (CPV): is a highly contagious viral illness affecting puppies and dogs, foxes, coyotes and wolves. Symptoms include vomiting, bloody diarrhoea, weight loss, and lack of appetite. Without prompt and proper treatment, dogs that have severe parvovirus infections can die within 48 to 72 hours.

Treatment will involve addressing dehydration and correcting electrolyte imbalances by administering intravenous fluids. Anti-inflammatory and antibiotic drugs are also given to control or prevent septicaemia, as well as drugs to control diarrhoea and vomiting.

Other Diseases and Viruses to Be Aware Of

What is Zoonotic? Zoonotic means a contagious disease that can be spread between both animals and humans.

Rabies: is a viral, zoonotic disease transmitted by coming into contact with the saliva of an infected animal, usually through a bite. The virus travels to the brain along the nerves and once symptoms develop (usually marked by a change in temperament), after a prolonged period of suffering, death is almost certainly inevitable. There is no treatment.

In most countries, vaccination against rabies is mandatory between the ages of twelve and sixteen weeks. If you plan to travel out of State or across country borders, you will need to make sure that your dog has an up-to-date Rabies Vaccination Certificate (NASPHV form 51) indicating they have been inoculated against rabies.

Leishmaniasis: is a contagious zoonotic infection caused by a parasite and is transmitted by a bite from a sand fly. While treatment involves the administration of a special drug (sodium stibogluconate), there is no definitive answer for effectively combating Leishmaniasis (especially since one vaccine will not prevent the known multiple species), with the prognosis often being fatal.

Symptoms include loss of appetite, diarrhoea, severe weight loss, exercise intolerance, vomiting, nosebleed, tarry feces, fever, pain in the joints, excessive thirst and urination, inflammation of the muscles, and death from kidney failure.

Lyme Disease: is one of the most common zoonotic tick-borne diseases in the world, which is transmitted by Borrelia bacteria found in the deer or sheep tick. Symptoms of this disease in a young or adult dog include recurrent lameness from joint inflammation, loss of appetite, depression, stiff walk with arched back, sensitivity to touch, swollen lymph nodes, fever, kidney damage, as well as rare heart or nervous system complications.

Control of the symptoms involves a lengthy course of antibiotic treatment in order to completely eliminate the organism.

Rocky Mountain Spotted Fever (RMSF): is a zoonotic disease transmitted by both the American dog tick and the RMSF tick, which must be attached to the dog for a minimum of five hours in order to transmit the disease.

Common symptoms include fever, reduced appetite, depression, painful joints, lameness, vomiting and diarrhoea, and some dogs may develop heart abnormalities, pneumonia, kidney failure, liver damage, or even neurological signs, such as seizures or unsteady, wobbly or stumbling gait. Treatment involves a 2-3 week course of antibiotics (Doxycycline or Tetracycline).

Ehrlichiosis: a tick-borne disease transmitted by both the brown dog tick and the Lone Star Tick, with common symptoms including depression, reduced appetite, fever, stiff and painful joints and bruising. The signs of infection typically occur less than a month after a tick bite and last for approximately four weeks. There is no vaccine available. Treatment involves a long course of antibiotics.

Anaplasmosis: deer ticks and Western blacklegged ticks are carriers of the bacteria that transmit canine Anaplasmosis. However, there is also another form of Anaplasmosis (caused by a different bacteria), that is carried by the brown dog tick.

Because the deer tick also carries other diseases, some animals may be at risk of developing more than one tick-borne disease at the same time. Signs are similar to Ehrlichiosis and include painful joints, diarrhoea, fever, and vomiting, as well as possible nervous system disorders. Treatment involves administering the antibiotic Doxycycline for a 30-day period.

Tick Paralysis: this zoonotic infection is caused when ticks attach themselves to the skin and secrete a neurotoxin that affects the nervous system. Affected dogs show signs of weakness and limpness approximately one week after being first bitten.

Symptoms usually begin with a change in pitch of the dog's usual bark, and weakness in the rear legs that eventually involves all four legs, followed by the dog showing difficulty breathing and swallowing. Your dog can die if not diagnosed and properly treated by removal of the tick.

Canine Coronavirus: this highly contagious intestinal disease, which is spread through the feces of contaminated dogs, while now found worldwide, can be destroyed by most commonly available disinfectants. Symptoms include diarrhoea, vomiting and weight loss or anorexia. There is a vaccine available, which is usually given to puppies, because they are more susceptible at a young age. This vaccine is also given to show dogs that have a higher risk of exposure to the disease.

Leptospirosis: is a worldwide zoonotic bacterial infection that can affect humans and many different kinds of animals, including dogs. If left untreated, there is potential for both dogs and humans to die from this disease.

The good news is that this virus is usually treated with antibiotics and supportive care, and because you can protect your dog with a vaccination, it makes sense to vaccinate against this disease if you and your dog live in an area considered a hot spot for leptospirosis.

Be aware that allergies can adversely affect your dog's health

One of the most common complaints discussed at the veterinarian's office when they see dogs obsessively scratching, biting, licking and chewing at their skin or paws is possible allergies, and there can be many triggers. When you educate yourself, you can help ensure your Beagle never has to suffer from allergies and can lead a healthier and happier life.

Environmental allergies: what many of us humans seem to forget is that our dogs can develop allergies to dust, chemicals, grass, mould, pollen, car exhaust, various forms of smoke, or flea and tick preparations, as well as allergies to materials such as wool or cotton, and chemicals found in washing soap or chemicals found in cleaning products you use around your home.

Visual symptoms are usually first noticed on the dog's stomach, inside of their legs, and at their tail or paws. Because many allergies are seasonal, our dogs will often be more affected in the spring or fall, with some airborne irritants inhaled by your dog resulting in coughing, sneezing or watery eyes.

Pay attention and if you think that your dog may have come in contact with an irritant found somewhere in your environment, first give them a cleansing bath, with the proper canine shampoo and conditioner.

Junk food allergies: *"True"* food allergies usually account for only about 10% of allergy problems in our canine friends.

Be aware that itching, chewing and chronic ear infections are not actually caused by food allergies, but rather are the result of a suppressed immune system, which is the result of your dog eating a low-quality diet. Food sensitivity issues can often be completely resolved by changing your dog's diet to a high-quality food that is more easily digested.

For instance, check food ingredients because far too many dog food products contain gluten ingredients that are common allergens to our fur friends, such as corn, wheat and soybeans. Become a label reader and ask questions, before you choose your dog's food.

Take the time to learn a little canine CPR

Of course, nobody wants to find his or herself in a situation where the life of their precious canine companion is put at risk. However, the reality is that accidents happen, and therefore knowing a little bit about how to help save your beloved furry friend is time well spent.

First of all, remember to handle an injured dog very carefully and gently. A dog that is traumatized, fearful or in pain, even one that is usually gentle, may lash out and try to bite.

Consider taking a class, because there are many animal CPR courses being offered these days through community educational systems or even online.

It's also a good idea to put together a canine first aid kit, both at home and in your vehicle, in case of emergencies, that includes the following items:

- Antiseptic Wash for wounds (hydrogen peroxide)
- Blanket
- Gauze Bandaging
- Kwik Stop styptic powder
- Medical Tape
- Nail Clippers
- Non-Stick Bandages for wounds

- Scissors
- Sterile Eye Wash
- Tick Twister
- Towel
- Tweezers
- Wash cloth

It would also be prudent to obtain a copy of the American Red Cross emergency techniques called *"Saving Your Pet With CPR"*, and familiarize yourself with the proper way to administer CPR to a dog.

<u>Artificial Respiration Step by Step</u>

If your dog becomes unconscious, depending upon what happened to them, they may stop breathing and if they stop breathing, they will go into cardiac arrest, when the heart stops beating and the dog dies.

However, after breathing stops, and before cardiac arrest, the heart can continue to beat for several minutes and this is when performing cardiopulmonary resuscitation (CPR) or artificial respiration can save your dog's life.

<u>Step 1</u>: place your dog on his or her side on a flat surface.

<u>Step 2</u>: check to make sure that your dog has actually stopped breathing by watching for the rise and fall of their chest and feel for their breath on your hand. Check the color of your dog's gums, because lack of oxygen will make them turn blue.

<u>Step 3</u>: check that the dog's airway is clear and there is nothing stuck in their mouth or throat by extending the head and neck and opening your dog's mouth.

If there is an object blocking their throat, pull the tongue outward and use your fingers or pliers to get a firm grip on the object so that you can pull it free from the dog's throat. If you cannot reach the object that appears to be blocking the dog's airway passage, you will have to use the Heimlich Manoeuver to try and dislodge it (see below).

Chapter 4: Healthy Beagle = Happy Dog

<u>Step 4</u>: so long as the dog's airway is not blocked, you can lift their chin to straighten out the neck and begin rescue breathing.

<u>Step 5</u>: hold the dog's muzzle and close their mouth, put your mouth over the dog's nose and blow gently – just enough to cause the dog's chest to rise.

<u>Step 6</u>: wait long enough for the air you just breathed into the dog's lungs to leave before giving another breath.

<u>Step 7</u>: continue giving one gentle breath every 3 seconds as long as the heart is still beating and until your dog starts to breathe on their own.

Canine Heimlich Manoeuvre

If breath won't go in, the airway may be blocked. In this case, you will need to turn your dog upside down, with his or her back held against your chest.

Wrap your arms around the dog and clasp your hands together just below the dog's rib cage (since the dog is being held upside down, this will be actually above the rib cage, in the abdomen).

Using both arms, give five sharp thrusts to the abdomen, and then check the dog's mouth or airway for the object. If the object is visible, remove it, and give two more rescue breaths.

CPR Step by Step

If your Beagle's heart has stopped beating, then CPR must be started immediately and ideal would be to have one person performing the artificial respiration, while the other performs the CPR.

<u>Step 1</u>: put your dog on his or her side on a flat surface.

<u>Step 2</u>: feel for your dog's pulse or heartbeat by placing one hand over his or her left side, just behind the front leg.

<u>Step 3</u>: place the palm of your hand on your dog's rib cage over his or her heart, with your other hand on top of the first (for puppies, put just your thumb on one side of the chest and the rest of your fingers on the other side).

Chapter 4: Healthy Beagle = Happy Dog

Step 4: press down and release, compressing the dog's chest approximately one inch (2-3 centimetres) and squeeze and release 80 to 100 times every minute.

While it's always the hope that you may never need to, if your dog is not breathing and there is no pulse, knowing what steps to take in an emergency (which includes how to do the doggy Heimlich Manoeuvre or apply compressions), could literally save the life of your own dog or maybe even someone else's.

In a Nutshell

While your dog may never suffer from any of the diseases known to occur in the Beagle breed, you will want to know what may afflict your dog because being aware of the signs can help them live a longer life. As well, familiarizing yourself with emergency CPR procedures in the following American Red Cross chart could help you save your dog's life.

It is also prudent to take the time to choose a veterinarian that can provide yearly check-ups, have your dog spayed or neutered in a timely fashion and educate yourself about required vaccinations.

Taking the steps outlined in this Chapter will help ensure that your Beagle will always have the best opportunity to be healthy and happy in your lifelong journey.

Chapter 4: Healthy Beagle = Happy Dog

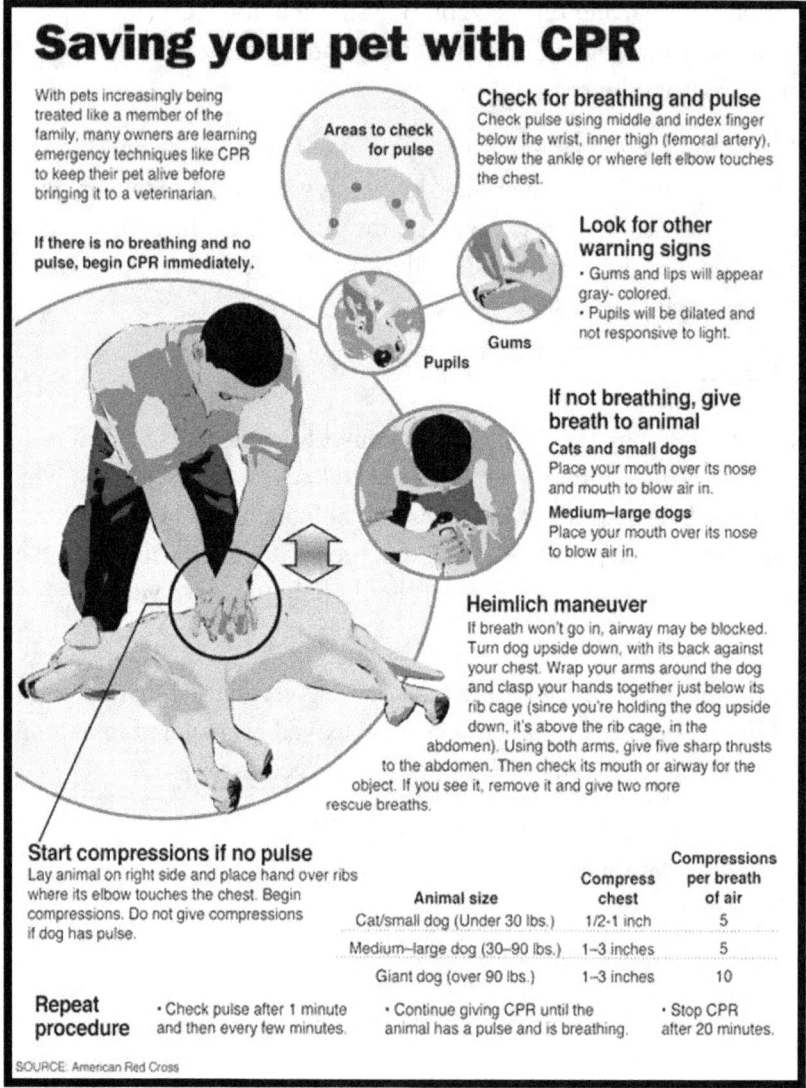

Chapter 5: Let Your Dog BE a Happy Dog

"Everyone thinks they have the best dog in the world. None of them are wrong."
— Unknown

This chapter is written to alert you to the fact that far too many of us humans have the tendency to treat our dogs more like human fur children than dogs.

You need to understand that not allowing your Beagle to be *"dog-like"* is very important when we're talking about THEIR happiness, because treating a dog like a human can ultimately result in <u>you</u> creating any number of behavioral issues.

Your Beagle is Not a Child

While this might sound like a strange Chapter title, there is no doubt that many humans simply don't allow their dogs to actually BE dogs, because they are too busy confusing their dog by attributing human emotions to them, and treating them like children.

Yes, some dogs may need to wear cute clothing to keep warm and dry, (such as the Beagle with their short and smooth coat), and depending on where they live, their guardian may need to provide them with protection from the cold and rain during the winter months. Also keep in mind that as this dog does not do particularly well in a warm climate, you will want to provide them with a cooling vest during warmer summer months when they are walking outside in the sunshine.

The Beagle has been developed as a companion for humans, which means that while this is not a dog that requires a great deal of exercise, some are more athletic and can enjoy participating in Frisbee or other canine sports, such as Agility or Flyball.

When your Beagle is a full-grown adult (approximately two years of age), you will definitely want to begin more complicated or advanced training sessions. They will enjoy it when you have the desire and patience, and they have the willingness.

If you and your Beagle are really enjoying learning new tricks together, you might want to advance to teaching them the hand signals for *"commando crawl"*, how to *"speak"* or to *"jump through the human hoop"*, or perhaps get them involved in a fun canine sport.

All of these tricks and many more are fun to teach and will exercise both mind and body, and the more control you have over your dog, the easier it will be to teach them a fun sport, such as Agility or Flyball.

The only restriction to how far you can go with training your adult Beagle will be your imagination and their personal ability or desire to perform.

Every dog has a uniquely wonderful set of gifts to share with their human counterparts, if only us humans would listen. They *"tell"* us when they are unhappy, frightened, bored, nervous, and when they are under-exercised, yet often we do not pay attention, or we just think they are being badly behaved.

Many humans today are deciding to have dogs instead of children and then attempting to manipulate their dogs into being small (or large) furry children. This is having a seriously detrimental effect upon the health, happiness and behavior of our canine companions.

Chapter 5: Let Your Dog BE a Happy Dog

Single, lonely people often have dogs, which is just fine, so long as the human side of the equation doesn't expect their canine counterpart to fulfill what humans require on an emotional level, because this is very confusing to a dog who needs their human to lead them.

In order to be the best guardians for our dogs, we humans must have a better understanding of what our dogs need from us, rather than what we need from them, so that they can live in safety, harmony and security within our human environment.

Sadly, many of us humans are not well equipped to give our dogs what they really need and that is why there are so many homeless, abandoned and frustrated dogs and so many overflowing rescue facilities.

As a professional dog whisperer who is challenged with the task of finding amicable solutions for canine/human relationships that have gone off the rails, I can tell you with certainty that once humans understand what needs to be changed and actually take the steps to do the work required, almost every stressful canine/human relationship can be turned into a happy one.

The sad part is that many humans are simply not willing or able to really understand the breed they are choosing, or willing or able to do the consistent work and devote the time necessary to ensuring that their chosen dog's needs are met.

Almost ALL canine problems, both mentally and physically, are a direct result of ignorance or unwillingness on the part of the human guardian to choose the right dog and then learn what their dog truly needs.

First and foremost, our dogs need to be respected for their unique canine qualities.

For millennia, dog has been considered *"Man's best friend"*. In today's society, when we want to do the best for our canine companions and create a harmonious relationship, we humans need to spend more time receiving the proper training WE need, so that we can learn how we humans can be dog's best friend.

Chapter 5: Let Your Dog BE a Happy Dog

Any dog can be your *"best friend"* providing that YOU educate yourself and put in the work, and this is a universal truth that applies to any canine breed, including the Beagle.

If you are considering this hard working and highly intelligent dog for your family, be certain that you can involve them in a wide variety of working tasks that will engage both their body and their mind, because doing so will ensure that you are raising a happy dog that never has to suffer from behavioral issues.

In a Nutshell

It's important to understand that you actually need to let your dog BE a dog if you want to raise a happy and healthy companion. While treating them like a fur covered child may be something YOU need, it's not what THEY need, and can create much confusion that often will lead to behavioral issues later in life.

Chapter 6: Every Happy Beagle Wants Exercise

*"Don't make the mistake of treating your dogs
like humans, or they'll treat you like dogs."*
— Martha Scott

While this breed requires a minimal daily physical al exercise regimen, they still need to go out for 2-3 on leash walks, walking properly at your side every day, because this will result in a strong bond of trust and respect between you that translates to both a healthy body and a healthy mind.

If you cannot commit to the time required to ensure the Beagle receives regular exercise each day, that engages both mind and body, this will soon be a very unhealthy, overweight, unhappy dog that could develop multiple health and behavior issues.

Before we outline what this dog's daily minimum and ideal exercise requirements should reasonably be, it may be helpful to first understand a little bit about what the Beagle was originally bred for and designed to do. This will give you some idea of what sorts of activities this comical clown dog will require when they are living as a companion within a human family.

Chapter 6: Every Happy Beagle Wants Exercise

Historical Origin of the Beagle

While most canine breeds have shrunk in size, the earliest Beagle was apparently much smaller than our modern-day Beagle. Exactly opposite to what has happened to so many older breeds that have been bred down in size, the Beagle has been bred larger.

The very early ancestors of the modern-day Beagle can be traced as far back as 5th century ancient Greece, and it is believed that the Beagle is descended from a mix of several breeds, including the North Country Beagle, the Southern Hound and the Talbot Hound. Some also believe that it is possible that the Beagle may contain some DNA from the Harrier breed, which resembles an English Fox Hound.

This small to medium-sized, excitable and loving canine was originally a working scent hound bred and developed in Great Britain during the 1830's for field tracking of both small and larger game, such as rabbits, hares and deer.

This canine, which used to be known as a *"Pocket Beagle"* or *"Miniature Beagle"* (now extinct) was approximately 8 or 9 inches (20 or 23 centimetres) high at the shoulder, which would have meant that they were indeed small enough to carry about in a pocket.

Queen Elizabeth I kept many of the now extinct, smaller *"Pocket Beagles"* that would fit into a pocket or saddlebag to ride along during a hunt. Once the larger hounds had located the prey, the smaller, pocket Beagles would continue the chase through dense underbrush.

Queen Elizabeth I called these smaller hounds her *"singing Beagles"* and they were permitted special privileges that sometimes involved entertaining her royal guests by allowing these small hounds to frolic across the plates and cups on the royal dining table.

After breeding Pocket Beagles with larger hunting hounds, the size of the breed gradually morphed into the larger form we recognize today as the Beagle.

Chapter 6: Every Happy Beagle Wants Exercise

The Beagle is a merry, social and enthusiastic dog that enjoys being in the midst of a large pack of dogs or spending time in a large family.

First recognized by the American Kennel Club in 1885, the Beagle has retained a top ten popularity ranking around the world for more than 30 years.

It is evident from the historical origins information above, that while the original ancestors of the Beagle were developed as hunting companions, (and while they may still retain their prowess in the field), this *"Foxhound in Miniature"* is more often seen being employed as a detection dog at airports, where these smaller hounds are used to sniff out food items in luggage, or enjoying life as a busy and affectionate family companion.

Minimum Daily Exercise Requirements

You will need to get your dog outside every day for a minimum of two or three 30 to 60 minute, on-leash, disciplined walks where they are walking at your side without pulling, and paying close attention to your commands.

Once properly leash trained, and heeding basic commands, the Beagle will also enjoy some off-leash freedom at a securely fenced local dog park where they can run, socialize, play with other dogs or retrieve a ball or Frisbee, so get into the habit of a daily visit to your local dog park or a trip to the beach or forest on one of your outings.

Keep in mind that this dog is **not** to be trusted off leash, as an interesting scent will start them howling and they will be off and running before you can turn around.

Ideal Daily Exercise Requirements

A fully-grown Beagle is an excitable and highly energetic dog with endless stamina that needs more daily exercise outside of the home than most humans are capable of providing. He or she will require both mental and physical stimulation from disciplined walks and plenty of daily exercise or canine sports in order to maintain a healthy weight.

Chapter 6: Every Happy Beagle Wants Exercise

This dog will need to burn off their daily pent up energy by going for at least three good walks of 30 minutes to an hour each beside their human companions every day, plus have an opportunity to run free chasing a ball or Frisbee or swimming to fetch a float or stick, or play amidst a pack of dogs, in a secure off-leash area. This dog cannot be trusted to roam freely off leash, as their wandering will soon have them disappearing over the next hill.

In order for this intelligent, friendly and enthusiastic dog to be happy and well balanced, they will want to be in middle of a large family. This means involving your Beagle in the family's activities and taking them everywhere with you, which also helps to socialize and exercise their brains and prevent them from becoming bored.

Leaving a loving and energetic dog home alone for many hours every day will be torture for them that could result in the Beagle making its own entertainment by becoming destructive and/or noisy by barking or howling.

The Beagle loves to run and has great stamina, and in order to maintain a healthy weight will require daily vigorous exercising. If this dog is permitted to become lazy and inactive, they will quickly gain weight, which can lead to problem health issues.

A very good way to give them the amount of exercise they really need is to train them to jog beside your bicycle. If you have access to a bicycle, consider training this dog to a *"Springer Bicycle Jogger"*, so that they can receive a good amount of disciplined, vigorous exercise in a short period of time.

Chapter 6: Every Happy Beagle Wants Exercise

The *"Springer Bicycle Jogger"* attachment for a bicycle is an ideal and safe way to adequately exercise this energetic dog while still keeping them under proper control, so that they cannot chase after a cat, squirrel or other distraction.

The Springer easily attaches to any bicycle and the arm can be quickly removed when not needed. The large spring attaches to a harness on the dog and there is a quick release, break-away tab at the top of the rope in case the dog runs around one side of a pole while you and the bike are on the other side. As well, the large spring in this arrangement ensures that if your dog tries to lunge or chase a squirrel, you and your bicycle will remain stable.

This is a dog that can be very excitable, who really needs a structured living situation and a regular exercise routine in order to prevent anxiety and other behavioral problems that may stem from being under-exercised.

Besides being an invaluable hunting partner, the Beagle can also be a serious competitor in several canine sports, such as Agility, show ring Conformation, Flyball, Trailing, Barn Hunt, or other Nose Work, and will also excel when being employed in the role of Detection and Sniffer Dog Services.

Ideal Living Conditions for a Happy Beagle

This merry character is as at home living on a farm as he or she would be in an apartment-sized space, so long as you make the effort to ensure that they get outside for their walks, play and socializing every day. However, they are more suited to living in a larger home environment.

Keep in mind that this is an excitable and highly energetic dog that needs plenty of daily exercise outside of the home.

While the Beagle was bred to be an active hunting companion, which means that they may have a strong urge to hunt small fleeing prey, such as rabbits or even the neighbor's cat, they are usually happy to greet strangers and friendly and peaceful with other pets.

Chapter 6: Every Happy Beagle Wants Exercise

This often stubborn and surprisingly athletic dog can get themselves out of seemingly inescapable crates, jump higher than you might imagine, climb fencing or dig and squeeze under a fence line or through a crack if an interesting scent catches their attention and they are feeling motivated.

Beagles are strongly connected to their guardians, and can often suffer from separation anxiety, which means that they really need to spend the majority of their time in the company of their humans. Therefore, if left alone in the back yard for long periods of time, and they can find a way to get out, be aware that there is a high likelihood that your dog may not be waiting for you when you return because he or she may have gone looking for you (or that interesting scent that caught their attention).

Whenever the slightest hint of food is involved, you need to keep a vigilant and watchful eye on this dog that may eat more than their share, which can lead to obesity.

You'll also find that it's very difficult to get upset with a dog that only wants to spend all of their time in your company, especially when they're gazing lovingly at you with those big appealing eyes and a sweet, soulful expression that could turn even the stoniest of hearts to mush.

The Beagle is sweet natured, loving companion who would do best in a home that includes a large, securely fenced back yard, where they can get outside to safely play and chase a ball with their humans.

Also, keep in mind that this yodelling escape artist will do what it takes to escape what others might consider to be the perfect back yard oasis; this is often because they want to be with their people (or any people) or they are simply under-exercised and bored and an intriguing scent makes its way to their specialized tracking nose.

This merry scent hound will dig under, jump over, or if they can get a foothold, scale a fence much higher than you would ever imagine possible. Also, don't think for a moment that just because you've put in the time to properly train your Beagle, that this will be enough to override their often strong desire to let their nose do the talking. This

Chapter 6: Every Happy Beagle Wants Exercise

dog is the master of *"selective hearing"*, and he or she will quickly lose interest in all else once an intriguing scent has grabbed their attention.

If you are unable to commit to providing the proper routine for this dog on a daily basis, that includes on-going socialization, training, and spending the majority of his or her time in your company, this merry mischief-maker will very likely first become unhealthily overweight, and second, may easily become nervous, anxious and suffer from separation anxiety. A dog that is suffering in this way, unlike some other behavioral issues, can take much patience and a very long time to turn around.

An under-exercised Beagle will become bored and unhappy, which can then cause them to develop behavioral problems that could include acting out in destructive ways by chewing furniture (or other *"off limits"* items in the home), ingesting non-food items (which can lead to emergency surgery or death), digging holes in the garden, escaping the back yard and ultimately suffering from anxiety and stress that can prematurely shorten their life..

In order to raise a happy Beagle that will be a contented member of your family, it will be essential that you provide him or her with vigorous daily disciplined walks and the opportunity for play time in the local park or competing in a fun canine sport (where they get to use their truly amazing sense of smell), in order to maintain a happy disposition and a healthy weight.

The best you can do for this sweet and fun-loving companion is to properly train, socialize and exercise them every day for longer than most humans are capable of (that's why you see so many fat Beagles) beginning from the time when you first bring them home from the breeders.

Above all else, never forget that all dogs are pack animals, which means that it is not normal for them to spend long periods of time by themselves, and this is even more important with a dog that has been bred to be a companion, such as the Beagle. When you adopt a dog into your family, you become their pack.

In other words, if you're planning to leave your Beagle alone for many hours every day, don't get a Beagle (or ANY dog for that matter), because you will be contributing to your fur friend developing a depressed and unhappy state of mind, and where the Beagle is concerned, most likely the stress of separation anxiety.

As well, when a bored Beagle has to find ways to entertain his or herself, you will also be opening the door to your loyal dog developing unwanted behaviors, such as becoming destructive, barking or yodelling until they become hoarse, or attempting to escape so they can wander the neighborhood in search of their humans or track a scent that can have them quickly covering many miles.

In a Nutshell

The bottom line here is that the Beagle is an affectionate, often stubborn, and always sweet and comical companion, with selective hearing when on a scent, that needs long, frequent walks every day. Taking the time to learn a little bit about this dog's original history will help you to better understand how important close interaction in combination with daily exercise and play will be for helping to keep this merry companion happy and healthy.

This Chapter also outlines different canine sports that a Beagle may excel at. Involving your dog in a sport is a great way to provide them with the exercise they need in a disciplined way that will engage their mind and help to ensure that your dog is a healthy and happy family member.

Take away Tip: while this dog needs a moderate to high amount of daily vigorous exercise, they also need <u>maximum</u> time in your company and will excel when you provide them with a daily routine that takes into consideration what is appropriate for their best physical and mental health.

Chapter 7: Feeding the Happy Beagle

*"Every dog lives for the day,
the hour, even the moment."*
— Robert Scott

It's not rocket science to grasp the concept that a properly fed Beagle means a healthy, happy and longer-lived companion, so make sure that you spend the time to research high-quality food and treats for your happy Beagle.

We are what we eat, and the same is absolutely true for our canine companions.

First, remember that our canine companions are carnivores, which means that they derive their energy and nutrient requirements and maintain their health by consuming a diet consisting mainly or exclusively of the flesh of animal tissues (in other words, meat).

When choosing an appropriate diet for your Beagle, considering the physiology of the canine's teeth, jaws and digestive tract will give you a better understanding of what food they should be eating.

Chapter 7: Feeding the Happy Beagle

Teeth, Jaws, and Digestive Tract

Teeth: canine teeth are all pointed because they are designed to rip, shred and tear into animal meat and bone.

Jaws: every canine is born equipped with powerful jaws and neck muscles for the specific purpose of being able to pull down and tear apart their hunted prey.

The jaw of every canine opens widely to hold large pieces of meat and bone, while the actual mechanics of the canine jaw permits only vertical (up and down) movement that is designed for crushing.

Digestive Tract: the canine digestive tract is short, simple and designed to move their natural choice of food (hide, meat and bone) quickly through their systems.

We humans need vegetables and plant matter in our diet and have the flat molars to effectively crush and chew them. While we often believe our dogs require the same, when choosing an appropriate food source for your Beagle, you need to consider that vegetables and plant matter require more time to break down in the gastrointestinal tract. This in turn, requires a more complex digestive system that the canine body simply does not have.

The canine digestive system is simply unable to break down vegetable matter, which is why whole vegetables look pretty much the same going into your dog, as they do coming out the other end.

Consider how much healthier and long-lived your beloved Beagle can be if, instead of largely ignoring nature's design for our canine companions, we chose to feed them whole, unprocessed, species-appropriate food.

Whatever you decide to feed your dog, keep in mind that, just as too much wheat or other grains and fillers in our human diet are having detrimental effects on our human health, the same can be very true for our dogs.

Chapter 7: Feeding the Happy Beagle

Read the labels so that you can be certain to avoid foods that contain fillers or high amounts of grains, because these are inappropriate for a healthy canine diet.

Control of Your Happy Beagle's Food

The Beagle will usually have a very healthy appetite, and their superior sense of smell will alert this dog to any potential food source, whether or not it's part of their usual diet. Conscientious guardians will need to carefully oversee the feed bowl and exactly what this dog puts in its mouth to ensure that he or she does not become overweight.

As this dog may be prone to eat too quickly, make sure that you purchase a slow feeder type of bowl for them to slow down the pace at which they can consume their food.

It's important that your Beagle understands that YOU are in control of their food source. Once they understand this, they will also figure that there will be windows of opportunity for receiving and eating their food, and this routine will help to develop healthy eating habits.

Many people use a scoop or measuring cup to put dry food into their dog's bowl. This is a mistake, because it's very important to mix your dog's food with your hands, so that your scent is all over the food, before you give it to them to eat. This sends a "message" to your dog that you are their pack leader, because it mimics what would happen if you were the alpha dog out hunting for your food in the wild.

For instance, while a pack of wild dogs hunting for food all work hard to capture their prey, the alpha pack leader always gets to eat first while all the other dogs must wait until the leader of the pack eats their fill, before they can rush in to eat what is left over.

Therefore, when you are mixing your domesticated dog's dinner with your hands, you are sending them the subtle message that you are the pack leader, you've already eaten your fill and you are now allowing them to eat what was left over.

Feeding Puppies

Chapter 7: Feeding the Happy Beagle

A general rule of thumb for growing Beagle puppies is to feed daily amounts of between 2 and 3% of what the puppy's adult weight is projected to be or 10% of the puppy's current body weight. You will want to keep in mind that while all puppies require extra protein during the first two years of their life to help them develop into healthy adult dogs, this is especially important with higher energy puppies.

There are now many foods on the market that are formulated for all stages of a dog's life (including the puppy stage). Whether you choose one of these foods or a food specially formulated for puppies, they will need to be fed smaller meals more frequently throughout the day (3 or 4 times), until they are at least one year of age.

Feeding Adults

Choose foods that list high-quality meat protein as the main ingredient and, depending on your dog's particular energy level, feed between 2 and 3% of their body weight every day. While some dogs prefer one meal a day, most will appreciate morning food (after a walk) and evening food (after a walk).

Be careful not to get caught up in "convenience" when you are out grocery shopping for yourself, and decide to buy your Beagle's food at the same place, because most grocery stores tend to carry inferior brands of dog food.

Instead, make the time to visit your local pet store, talk with educated representatives, avoid grains, and choose quality sources of meat protein for healthy puppies and dogs, including beef, buffalo, chicken, duck, fish, hare, lamb, ostrich, pork, rabbit, turkey, venison, or any other source of wild meaty protein.

Treats

There are endless choices of dog treats lining the shelves of every feed store, pet store, and grocery store, and it will be an overwhelming task to choose wisely, unless you keep one simple rule in mind, and choose treats that contain only one ingredient or very few ingredients.

Chapter 7: Feeding the Happy Beagle

Whatever reason you choose to give treats to your Beagle, keep in mind that if we treat our dogs too often throughout the day, they can become overweight, and we may create a picky eater who will no longer want to eat their regular meals.

As well, researchers in Sweden have discovered that dogs were happier when they had to earn their treats as a reward for completing a task, rather than just being given a treat for looking cute, because just like us humans who get that happy "eureka" moment when we finally solve a problem, the same is true for our canine counterparts. The Beagle is the perfect dog for positive training methods that involve treat reinforcement.

Dangerous Treats

Always carefully read labels and take note of where treats are manufactured, because not all countries have the most stringent manufacturing protocols, and honestly there are many treats that you absolutely should NOT be feeding your dog, including:

Rawhide, which is soaked in an ash/lye solution to remove every particle of meat, fat and hair and then further soaked in bleach to remove remaining traces of the ash/lye solution. Now that the product is no longer food, it no longer has to comply with food regulations.

The wet rawhide is shaped into chews, and once dry it shrinks to approximately 25% of its original size before arsenic-based products are used as preservatives, and antibiotics and insecticides are added to kill bacteria.

While rawhide chews are tough and long lasting, when a dog chews a rawhide treat, they ingest many harsh chemicals. Also, when your dog swallows a piece of rawhide, that piece can swell up to four times its size inside your dog's stomach, which can cause anything from mild to severe gastric blockages that could become life threatening and require surgery.

Pig's Ears are very attractive to most dogs that will eagerly devour them. However, they are thin, crispy and very high in fat, which can

Chapter 7: Feeding the Happy Beagle

cause stomach upsets, vomiting and diarrhoea. In addition, pieces can break off and become stuck in a dog's throat.

Also, pig ears are often processed and preserved with unhealthy chemicals that discerning dog guardians will not want to feed their dogs.

Hoof Treats are actual cow, horse and pig hooves that humans believe are healthy, *"natural"* treat choices for their dogs when the truth is that after processing with harsh chemicals, preservatives and antibiotics, they retain little, if any, of their *"natural"* qualities.

Also, hooves are very hard and can cause the chipping or breaking of your dog's teeth as well as perforation or blockages in your dog's intestines.

Healthy Treats

There are so many healthy treat choices available, which means that there is no excuse for feeding your Beagle unhealthy, nutrient-deficient treats. Read the labels to make sure the treats you are choosing are appropriately sized for your dog and are of the highest quality. Examples of healthy treats include:

Hard Treats: come in many varieties of shapes, sizes and flavors and will help to keep your dog's teeth cleaner.

Soft Treats: are also available in endless varieties and flavors, suitable for all the different needs of our furry friends and are often smaller in size and used for training purposes.

Dental Treats or Chews: are designed with the specific purpose of helping your dog to maintain healthy teeth and gums by exercising the jaw and massaging gums, while removing plaque build-up near the gum line.

Freeze-Dried and Jerky Treats: offer a tasty morsel most dogs find irresistible as they are usually made of simple, meaty ingredients, such as liver, poultry and seafood. Be careful when choosing jerky treats, as they are often processed with too much salt.

Human Food Treats: be very careful when feeding human foods to dogs as treats, because many of our foods contain unhealthy additives, such as salt, sugar and other ingredients that could be toxic and harmful.

Also, educate yourself about the common human foods that are actually poisonous to our canine friends, such as grapes, raisins, onions and chocolate, to name a few.

Generally, the treats you feed your dog should not make up more than approximately 10% of their daily food intake, so make sure the treats you choose are high quality, with single or few ingredients so that you can help to keep your Beagle both happy and healthy.

The Right Food for Your Happy Beagle

"Dog Food" has significantly changed since 1785, when the English Sportman's Dictionary described the best diet for a dog's health in an article entitled *"Dog"*. This article indicated that the best food for a dog was something called *"Greaves"*, described as "*the sediment of melted tallow made into cakes for dogs' food*".

From these meager beginnings, commercially manufactured dog food has become a massively lucrative industry that has only fairly recently evolved beyond feeding our dogs the dregs of human leftovers, because it was cheap and convenient for us.

Even today, the majority of dog food choices often have far more to do with being convenient for humans to store and serve, than it does with being a diet truly designed to be a nutritionally balanced, healthy food choice for our canine companions.

Educating yourself by talking to experts and reading everything you can find on the subject, plus taking into consideration several relevant factors, will help to answer the dog food question for you and your dog.

For instance, where you live may dictate what sorts of foods you have access to, while other factors to consider will include the particular requirements of your dog, such as their age, energy and activity levels.

Chapter 7: Feeding the Happy Beagle

Our dogs are also suffering from many of the same life-threatening diseases that are commonly found in our human society (heart disease, cancer, diabetes, obesity). These diseases all have a direct correlation with over-feeding and/or eating genetically altered foods that are no longer pure, in favor of a convenient, processed and packaged diet that is quick and easy for us to serve.

The Raw Diet: raw feeding advocates believe that the ideal diet for their dog is one which would be very similar to what a dog living in the wild would have access to while hunting or foraging.

These canine guardians are often opposed to feeding their dog any sort of commercially manufactured pet foods, because they consider them to be poor substitutes, and for the most part, I would agree.

For instance, many guardians of high energy, working breed dogs will agree that their dogs thrive on a raw or BARF (Biologically Appropriate Raw Food) diet and strongly believe that the potential benefits of feeding a raw dog food diet are many, whether your dog is earning a daily working wage or simply being your loyal companion, including:

- Healthy, shiny coats
- Decreased shedding
- Fewer allergy problems
- Healthier skin
- Cleaner teeth
- Fresher breath
- Increased energy levels
- Improved digestion
- Smaller stools
- Strengthened immune system

Chapter 7: Feeding the Happy Beagle

- Increased mobility in arthritic pets
- Increase or improvement in overall health

A raw diet is a direct evolution of what dogs ate before they became our domesticated pets and we turned toward commercially prepared, easy-to-serve dry dog food that required no special storage or preparation.

The Dehydrated Diet: is available in both raw and cooked meat forms, which are usually air dried to reduce moisture and inhibit bacterial growth. While the appearance of dehydrated dog food is very similar to dry kibble, the typical feeding methods include adding warm water before serving, which makes this type of diet both healthy for our dogs and convenient for us to serve.

Dehydrated recipes are made from minimally processed fresh, whole foods to create a healthy and nutritionally balanced meal that retains more of the overall nutritional value, and will meet or exceed the dietary requirements of a healthy canine.

A dehydrated diet is a convenient way to feed your dog a nutritious diet, because all you have to do is add warm water and wait five minutes while the food re-hydrates so your dog can enjoy a warm meal.

The Kibble Diet: there is no mistaking that the convenience and relative economy of dry dog food kibble, which had its beginnings in the 1940's, continues to be the most popular pet food choice for many dog-friendly humans. Thankfully, there are now many high-quality kibble foods available.

The Right Bowl for the Beagle: there are many different types and categories of dog bowls, including Automatic Watering, Elevated, Ceramic, Stoneware, No Skid, No Tip, Slow Feeder, Stainless, Wooden and Travel Bowls.

Keeping in mind that your Beagle will usually be highly food motivated and may wolf their food, you will definitely want to get this dog a slow feeder type of bowl to help slow them down when they eat.

Chapter 7: Feeding the Happy Beagle

<u>In a Nutshell</u>

While food and treat choices for your favorite furry Beagle can be overwhelming, a basic understanding of canine physiology and making wise decisions concerning all the many different types of food available, will help you to add many healthy and happy years to your dog's life.

You are the sole protector of your canine companion, and I cannot stress strongly enough the importance of a well thought out choice when deciding what brand and type of food you will feed your loyal Beagle.

Appropriate food and treat choices can not only increase the length of your dog's life by avoiding unwanted health conditions, such as obesity, high blood pressure or bladder stones, but good food choices will also provide your dog with optimal health so they can feel good and live a happy life!

Chapter 8: Care of the Happy Beagle

*"If you think a dog can't count,
try putting three dog biscuits in your pocket,
and then give him only two of them."*
— Phil Pastoret

Imagine you're travelling by car on a daily basis without being protected by a seatbelt or an airbag. How safe would you feel? Unfortunately, this is the reality for lots of our furry friends, because their guardians have neglected their safety responsibilities.

Now, imagine going for months without washing your hair, cutting your nails or brushing your teeth. Again, that is the reality for many dogs, because their owners have not been advised with respect to the importance of good grooming. How happy and well-behaved do you think such an ill-cared for dog would be?

The following few paragraphs outline safe travelling, licensing, insurance and grooming requirements, all of which can help to ensure that your Beagle is safe, legal and better cared for at the vet's office.

Keep in mind that if your Beagle is safely secured when travelling, they might not be dead or seriously injured should you be involved in a

Chapter 8: Care of the Happy Beagle

vehicle accident. We humans wear seatbelts to be safe – what about safety for our best fur friends?

Further, if your dog is properly licensed, they will be returned to you should they go missing, and this is a much happier dog than one spending who knows how long behind bars at a rescue or SPCA.

As well, if you have pet health insurance, chances are that they will be better cared for at the vet's office, which means a healthier and happier dog.

Tips for Keeping Your Dog Safe

Not So Safe Harness Restraints: is your canine companion safe when buckled into a safety harness for travel in vehicles? Be aware that many of the dog harnesses in the marketplace have a 100% failure rate.

If you cannot find a safety harness that is actually been strength tested and crash tested (i.e. optimal choice), the safest travel arrangement for any dog is to secure them inside a kennel, that is bolted to the floor or secured with the vehicles seatbelt.

Kennels: a dog kennel or crate will easily fit (sideways) on the back seat of most vehicles and can be secured with the vehicle's restraint system. A Beagle riding inside a kennel that is secure inside your vehicle will have the best protection in the case of a rollover accident, plus you will avoid the fines some locations are now levying for allowing a dog to roam freely inside a moving vehicle.

Air Travel: while the Beagle puppy (depending on age) may be small enough to fit into a soft Sherpa bag for travel inside an airplane cabin (as carry-on baggage), they will usually be too large to travel inside the airplane cabin when they are fully grown, and will need to be transported inside a heated cargo hold.

Licensing: when you purchase your dog a yearly license or identifying tag, they will be legal, and should they become lost when wearing a license, there is a much higher possibility that your dog will be returned to you, instead of spending their last few days behind bars at the local SPCA or rescue facility.

Pet Health Insurance: purchasing health insurance for your dog means that they will usually live a longer, healthier and happier life, because they will receive better care throughout their lifetime.

Be aware that you need to begin insurance when your dog is a young puppy, because waiting until they are older will mean that your monthly premiums are considerably higher.

Grooming Your Dog

Regular grooming is important for a happy and healthy Beagle, because it keeps them clean, their skin moisturized and bug free, plus grooming time can alert you to any problems before they become more serious.

Unless you are paying someone else to professionally groom your dog, there will be a basic arsenal of equipment and products you will need to purchase so that you can keep your happy Beagle looking his or her best.

Also, you will want to get your dog used to their grooming routine early on, because otherwise, every time your dog needs to be groomed will end up being a traumatic experience for both dog and human that can last for many years. Start them off right so you can both enjoy grooming time.

For instance, I've been asked to groom dogs that have been kicked out of every grooming salon because their owners did not take the time to introduce the puppy to bath time, nail clipping and other necessary grooming procedures at a young age.

I can tell you from much personal experience that having to groom a writhing, screaming dog that is all teeth, because they are fighting the procedure, is hell on wheels. Try going through this with an unwilling, sturdy Beagle and you will very soon be wishing your companion were a chia pet.

Grooming Equipment You Will Need

A standard arsenal of equipment that will help you keep your Beagle looking their best will include a brush to remove all that shedding dead

Chapter 8: Care of the Happy Beagle

hair and help distribute natural oils, a pair of nail clippers, and a flea comb and tick twister (just in case).

A bristle brush – is the ideal tool for removing debris and dead hair from the Beagle's coat, while at the same time distributing natural oils to keep the coat looking healthy and shiny.

Nail clippers or scissors (and/or a slow speed pet Dremel™) – will be tools you need to use every couple of weeks or more, depending on how quickly your Beagle's nails grow and what types of surfaces they may be walking on.

Flea comb – hopefully you won't ever need one, however, as the name suggests, these combs are designed for the specific purpose of removing fleas from a dog's coat. Usually small in size for manoeuvring in tight spaces, they may be made of plastic or metal with the teeth of the comb placed very close together to trap hiding fleas.

Tick Twister – hopefully your dog won't ever get a tick, but if they do, this is a simple device for painlessly, easily and quickly removing ticks that have imbedded themselves in your dog's skin.

Grooming Products You Will Need

Products you will need to invest in when grooming your dog yourself will include shampoos, conditioners, creams, lotions, sprays and powders.

Shampoos: NEVER make the mistake of using human shampoo or conditioner that has a pH balance of 5.5, for bathing your dog. Our canine companions have an almost neutral pH balance of 7.5, and any shampoo with a lower pH will be harmful to your dog, because it will strip the natural oils and be too harshly acidic for their coat and skin, which can create itchy skin problems and allow for a very unhappy dog.

Conditioners: taking the extra time to condition your Beagle's coat will not only make it look and feel better, it will also add additional benefits, including:

- Preventing the escape of natural oils and moisture

Chapter 8: Care of the Happy Beagle

- Keeping the coat cleaner for a longer period of time
- Repairing a coat that has become dull, damaged or dry
- Restoring a soft, silky feel
- Helping the coat dry more quickly
- Protecting from the heat of the dryer and breakage of hair

The benefits of spending the extra two minutes to condition your dog's coat will be appreciated by both yourself and your dog that will have overall healthy, moisturized skin and a coat with a natural shine.

Oops, My Dog Has Fleas

You haven't been paying attention and now realize that your dog is suffering from an infestation of fleas. Now is the time to bathe them with shampoo containing pyrethrum (a botanical extract found in small, white daisies) or a shampoo containing citrus or tea tree oil.

Also, you can bathe and spray them with the non-toxic and highly effective CedarCide products, which can also be used to spray down their bedding and any carpets in the home, and will kill fleas (or other crawly creatures) on contact without harming anyone.

CedarCide is a company that makes 100% safe, organic products to control biting bugs on your furry friends without worrying about harmful chemicals that are not good for you, your children or your canine companions.

Simply spray it on and bugs of any sort that come into contact with the solution will be dead, while your dog's coat will be shiny and fresh smelling, like the inside of a cedar chest.

Nail Care

Many canine guardians neglect taking proper care of their dog's toenails, which can lead to many problems later in life, such as painful joints and difficulty walking, which will make for a very unhappy Beagle.

Chapter 8: Care of the Happy Beagle

Purchase a good pair of clippers and learn how to properly use them every two to three weeks.

Styptic Powder: you will always want to avoid causing any pain when trimming your Beagle's toenails, because you don't want to destroy their trust in you regularly performing this necessary task.

However, accidents do happen, therefore if you clip too short, and accidentally cut into the vein in the toenail, know that you will cause your dog pain, and that the toenail will bleed. Therefore, it is always a good idea to keep some styptic powder (often called *"Kwik Stop"*) in your grooming kit.

Dip a moistened finger into the powder and apply it with pressure to the end of the bleeding nail, because this is the quickest way to stop a nail from bleeding in just a few seconds.

Some dogs prefer having their nails trimmed with a rotary "Dremel" type of device that grinds down the excess nail and with this tool, it is easier to avoid cutting into the vein. Keep in mind that if you decide to trim your dog's nails this way, you will have to purchase a *"doggy Dremel"* made especially for this purpose, because using your shop Dremel will harm your dog's nails as it is too high speed and will burn the nails.

Ear Care

Dogs can often suffer from painful ear infections, especially those with long, hanging ears (like the Beagle), because these ears can easily retain moisture.

Paying attention and keeping your dog's ears clean and dry will prevent this type of unhappy pain and suffering. Make sure that you keep ear powders and cleaning solutions in your grooming kit, because with proper preventative care, your dog need never suffer from an ear infection.

Ear Powders: which can be purchased at any pet store, are designed to help keep your dog's ears dry while at the same time inhibiting the growth of bacteria that can lead to infections. Ear powders are also used

Chapter 8: Care of the Happy Beagle

when removing excess hair growth from inside a dog's ear canal, as the powder makes it easier to grip the hair.

Ear Cleaning Solutions: your local pet store will offer a wide variety of ear cleaning creams, drops, oils, rinses or wipes specially formulated for cleaning your Beagle's ears.

In addition, there are many home remedies that will just as efficiently clean your dog's ears without the high price tag, including Witch Hazel (a 50:50 solution of Organic Apple Cider Vinegar and Purified Water) or a 50:50 solution of Hydrogen Peroxide and Purified Water.

Teeth Care

Another greatly overlooked area in your happy Beagle's health is ensuring that their teeth are clean and properly looked after, so that they don't suffer from loose or broken teeth, and plaque build-up that leads to painful gum disease. You know how miserable a toothache can be – imagine your poor dog that cannot tell you how unhappy they are.

Many guardians use the excuse that *"my dog doesn't like it"* when they try to brush their dog's teeth, and overlook the fact that in order to keep their entire dog healthy, they <u>must</u> have healthy teeth and the only way to ensure this, is to commit to making the time to brush your dog's teeth every day.

Canine Toothpastes: are flavoured with beef or chicken in an attempt to appeal to the dog's taste buds, while some contain baking soda, which is the same mild abrasive found in many human pastes, and are designed to gently scrub the teeth.

Other types of canine toothpastes are formulated with enzymes that are designed to work chemically by breaking down tartar or plaque in the dog's mouth. While these pastes don't need to be washed off your dog's teeth and are safe for them to swallow, whether or not they remain on the dog's teeth long enough to do any good might be debatable.

Just as effective for killing germs, whitening and cleaning your dog's teeth, and much less expensive than fancy pastes, is old-fashioned hydrogen peroxide; you can combine hydrogen peroxide (3% food grade), Aloe Vera juice (1:1) with a little bit of baking soda.

Paw Care

If your dog runs over sharp barnacles on the beach, jogs with you on hard road surfaces, or over other rough surfaces, this can cause cuts and scrapes and very rough surfaces on the paws. If you live in a hot climate, be aware that sidewalks, road surfaces and sandy beaches can get extremely hot for your Beagle's feet.

Paw Creams: depending upon activity levels and the types of surfaces our canine counterparts usually walk on, they may suffer from cracked or rough pads. You can restore resiliency and keep your dog's paws in healthy condition by regularly applying a cream or lotion to protect their paw pads. A good time to do this is just after you've clipped their nails.

In a Nutshell

Learning about simple steps that will keep your Beagle safe, and what's involved in keeping him or her properly groomed will go a long way toward helping them to live a long, happy and healthy life.

While for many people the concept of grooming your dog conjures up notions of brushes and bows, it is in fact a vital element to their overall health and wellbeing.

Regularly grooming your dog will help you detect any underlying diseases or conditions early and will allow your beloved fur friend to feel better and live longer and happier.

Chapter 9: Are YOU the Ideal Happy Beagle Guardian?

"Happiness is a warm puppy."
— Charles M. Schulz

If you have not chosen wisely when sharing your life with a canine companion, you are setting yourself, your family, your friends and your neighbours up for many years of stress, guilt and unhappiness.

It is vitally important that you take a good hard look at your own energy level and lifestyle, ask yourself some serious questions that you honestly answer, and not scrimp on taking the time to do plenty of research about the breed of dog you may be considering.

Sharing your life with a canine friend should never be undertaken lightly, or on a whim or spur of the moment decision, or because you like the colour of a dog's coat or the sweet expression on their face.

Before you can learn how to become your dog's ideal guardian, you need to first have no doubt in your mind that you have the energy, commitment, time and skill level necessary to raise a happy dog. Once this is established in the affirmative, you then need to know how to choose the right breed of puppy or dog.

Chapter 9: Are YOU the Ideal Happy Beagle Guardian?

Choosing the <u>right</u> puppy for your family and your lifestyle is more important than you might imagine, and far too many people forget to consider how important is to choose a puppy or dog based on compatibility with their own energy and lifestyle.

For instance, many humans choose a puppy (or older dog) for all the <u>wrong</u> reasons, including because:

- they like what it looks like
- the breed may currently be popular
- the breed appeared on TV or in a movie they enjoyed
- their parents had the same kind of dog when they were a child
- a friend has the same breed
- they feel sorry for a homeless dog
- a friend or family member can no longer keep their dog
- the children are begging for a dog
- someone was selling puppies on a street corner

While some of these above reasons can be honourable, the most important reasons for choosing to share your life with a particular canine companion has not been properly considered.

In order to make an intelligent choice that will bring happiness to everyone, you need to take a serious look at your life as it is today and also how you envision it to be during the next ten to fifteen years, and then ask yourself several very important questions, including:

Activity – Do I lead a highly active, medium or low-intensity life? For instance, am I out jogging the streets every morning, hiking local mountains or riding my bicycle five miles to the local grocery store, or does my job or leisure time activity keep me in front of the computer or on the couch watching movies?

Travel – Do I travel a lot for work or pleasure? If you do, perhaps you should choose a small dog that can travel with you in the plane cabin; your loyal dog will be unhappy without you or you will have greatly

Chapter 9: Are YOU the Ideal Happy Beagle Guardian?

increased expenses, because you will have to hire a dog sitter or leave them in a kennel.

Allergies – Do I prefer a very tidy house? Do I have allergies? Many breeds, like the Beagle, shed their hair all year round and your entire house and everything you own will be covered with dog hair. This means more frequent housework and if you or your family members have allergies, as much as they may enjoy the company of a furry friend, if you decide to proceed, better would be to choose a non-shedding breed.

Time – Does my family take up all my spare time and are my children old enough to handle a puppy? A dog is like a child that never grows up and in order for them to be happy and well-behaved family members, they require a lot of your daily time and attention.

Fitness – Am I physically fit and healthy enough to be out there walking a dog two to three times a day, every day, rain or shine, and much more during the puppy stage? Do I have the time to involve them in a canine sport or job?

Cost – Am I able to afford the extra food costs, health insurance, licensing, appropriate clothing and the veterinarian expenses that are part of being a conscientious Beagle guardian?

Commitment – Is the decision to bring a puppy or dog into my life a family decision, or just because the children, who may quickly lose interest, have been begging for a dog?

Why? – What is the number one reason why I want a dog in my life?

Once you ask yourself these important questions and honestly answer them, you will have a much better understanding of whether you have what it takes to share your life with a dog, and perhaps the beginning insight of the type of puppy or dog that would be best suited for you and your family.

If you're too busy for a dog, or choose the wrong dog that is not compatible with you or your family's energy and lifestyle (or you don't really have the time and commitment necessary to properly socialize,

Chapter 9: Are YOU the Ideal Happy Beagle Guardian?

train, exercise, and raise a canine companion), you will inevitably end up with an unhappy dog, which will lead to behavioral issues, which then will lead to a stressed family, angry neighbors, and in a best case scenario, extra expenses to hire a professional to help you reverse unwanted behavioral problems.

Even worse, an incompatible choice can mean that you may end up contributing to the already overflowing crisis of another dog being abandoned at the local SPCA or kill shelter.

Once you have done all your homework, and absolutely determined that the Beagle is the right dog for you (see next Section: The Ideal Guardian), rather than simply leaving it to chance, you need to choose the right puppy from the litter.

Generally speaking, when choosing a puppy out of a litter, look for one that is friendly and outgoing, rather than one who is overly aggressive or fearful.

Visit the breeder and take note of a puppy's social skills when they are still with their littermates, because this will help you to choose the right puppy for your family. Puppies who demonstrate good social skills with their littermates are much more likely to develop into easy-going, happy adults who play well with other dogs.

In a social setting where all the puppies can be observed together, there are several important observations you can make, including:

Play – Notice which puppies are comfortable both on top and on the bottom when play fighting and wresting with their littermates, and which puppies seem to only like being on top. Puppies who don't mind being on the bottom or who appear to be fine with either position will usually play well with other dogs when they become adults.

Sharing – Observe which puppies try to keep the toys away from the other puppies and which puppies share. Those who want to hoard the toys and keep all other puppies away may be more aggressive with other dogs over food or treats, or in play where toys are involved as they become older.

Company – Notice which puppies seem to like the company of the other pups and which ones seem to be loners. Puppies who like the company of their littermates are more likely to be interested in the company of other dogs as they mature than anti-social puppies.

Compassion – Observe the reaction of puppies that get yelped at when they bite or roughhouse with another puppy too hard. Puppies who ease up when another puppy yelps or cries are more likely to respond appropriately when they play too roughly as adults.

Sociability – Check to see if the puppy you are interested in is sociable with people, because if they will not come to you, or display fear of strangers, this may develop into a fear/aggression problem when they become adults.

Handling – Check if the puppy you are interested in is relaxed about being handled, because if they are not, they may become difficult or overly nervous around adults and children during daily interactions, during grooming or while visiting the veterinarian's office.

Is Your Happy Puppy Healthy?

While mental health is very important, you will also want to do all you can to determine if your chosen puppy is physically healthy.

First, ask to see veterinarian reports from the breeder to satisfy yourself that the puppy is as healthy as possible, and then once you make your decision to share your life with a particular puppy, and they are old enough to bring home, make an appointment with your own veterinarian for a complete examination.

However, before you take your new puppy home, there are general signs of good health to be aware of, including the following:

Body Fat – a healthy puppy will look round and well fed, with an obvious layer of fat over their rib cage.

Breathing – a healthy puppy will breathe quietly, without coughing, wheezing or sneezing.

Chapter 9: Are YOU the Ideal Happy Beagle Guardian?

Coat Condition – a healthy puppy will not be itchy and will have a soft coat with no dandruff, dullness, greasiness or bald spots.

Energy Level – a well-rested puppy will be alert and energetic.

Hearing – a healthy puppy should react if you clap your hands or snap your fingers behind their head.

Genitals – a healthy puppy will not have any sort of discharge visible in or around their genital or anal regions.

Mobility – a healthy puppy will walk and run normally without wobbling, limping or seeming to be weak, stiff or sore.

Vision – a healthy puppy will have bright, clear eyes without crust or discharge and they should notice if a ball is rolled past or a toy is tossed within their field of vision.

The Ideal Guardian

Once you have established that you have what it takes to share your life with a dog (by considering the questions in the previous Section), you should consider the following tips to determine whether the Beagle would be the right breed for you and your family.

The Beagle will be an excellent choice for high-energy individuals or families with older children as they are friendly, sweet natured and playful. This dog can also be a good companion for senior adults who have the energy, time and mobility required to provide this dog with the vigorous daily exercise and mental stimulation they need.

Keep in mind that while a well-socialized Beagle will usually be accepting of both unknown dogs and humans, when not trained to heed their guardian's every word, they can be stubborn and decide to be the boss, and this can lead to unwanted problems.

The ideal guardian for the Happy Beagle will be a person (or family) who is retired or works at home, and enjoys several long and vigorous daily walks. This guardian will also be aware of this dog's superior sense of smell and how easily they can become distracted, which means that they are not to be trusted off leash where they can quickly

Chapter 9: Are YOU the Ideal Happy Beagle Guardian?

disappear. This ideal guardian will also understand the basics of socializing and training, and may also enjoy teaching this companion a fun canine sport or be willing to involve this canine companion in their own daily hiking, jogging or biking routine.

As an example, the ideal happy Beagle guardian will be someone who works at home or is retired, and takes his or her dog out for a vigorous, long walk first thing every morning before breakfast.

After returning home, everyone will have their breakfast and then (since you work at home or are retired) your dog can rest for a couple of hours while you work about the home. Depending on the weather, before long it's noon and time to leash up your energetic companion and head off for another long walk, where you may finish up at a securely fenced local dog park for a game of ball or play with other dogs.

Back home for a midday snack for your dog and lunch for you, while you take time (depending on this dog's age) to teach basic commands, or maybe some tricks before your dog has a snooze and you get back to your time at home.

Now it's about 4:00 pm and again it's time to get you and your dog outside for a 30 to 60-minute walk and if it's not too hot or too cold out, perhaps another short play at the park.

Back home and time to prepare dinner for both dog and human, then after dinner (again depending on the age of your dog) perhaps a few more minutes of basic command and/or trick training before you each have some lazy time in front of the fire or TV screen.

Now it's getting to be later evening and before bed you need to put your Beagle on leash and take them outside for a quick walk around the block, so they can drain out their bladder before bed.

Everyone now in his or her respective beds as both human and dog have a rejuvenating sleep before the start of the next day when you do this all over again.

Chapter 9: Are YOU the Ideal Happy Beagle Guardian?

Of course, this is just one scenario that would be excellent for the Happy Beagle, and with a little imagination on your part, there are many others that would fit the bill quite nicely.

For instance, if you have access to a bicycle, one of your 30 to 60 minute walks might be a bike ride with your Beagle hitched up to a jogger so they can run beside you.

Also, don't forget to check out your local weekend canine sporting facilities, and take the time to get you and your dog involved, because your weekend would be well spent teaching this dog how to run an Agility course, get involved in the sport of Barn Hunt or Tracking, or perhaps participate in an Advanced Obedience competition or strut their stuff around the Show ring.

In a Nutshell

While learning how to choose the right puppy is important, even more important is your ability to ask and honestly answer the questions outlined in this Chapter that will help you to understand if you truly are a good fit for being the ideal guardian for the high energy Beagle.

If you don't really have the time and commitment necessary to properly socialize and raise this sweet-natured, friendly companion, you will inevitably end up with an unhappy dog, which will lead to health and behavioral issues, which then will lead to a stressed family, angry neighbors, and extra expenses to hire a professional to help you reverse unwanted behavioral problems.

Chapter 10: Humans Make a LOT of Stupid Mistakes

"A house is not a home until it has a dog."
— Gerald Durrell

Far too often we humans don't even realize we are the cause of creating behavioral problems in our canine companions, and when we are not aware and paying attention, we may be causing a lot of issues that can actually be entirely avoided.

Besides the more obvious problems that can arise with a dog that is bred for tracking, hunting or other detection work and can become a unhappy member of your family when not raised properly (and adequately exercised), there are many other situations or unwanted outcomes that may arise that can be avoided.

For instance, not taking the time to properly socialize your Beagle, forgetting about desensitizing them to loud noises, accidentally rewarding them at the wrong time, or not taking the time to teach basic rules and boundaries, can all lead to plenty of trouble in later life and create unhappiness and unwanted behavior issues.

Chapter 10: Humans Make a LOT of Stupid Mistakes

As well, not being aware of the adolescent craziness time in a dog's life and how to get through it, and many other less obvious mistakes, such as choosing the wrong collar or leash, sleeping in your bed, or free feeding can all result in the creation of problems.

While we humans may be well meaning, besides the obvious disasters that we can create when we don't properly train or socialize our canine friends, we can inadvertently make a lot of stupid mistakes when raising our canine companions that will cause our fur friends to needlessly suffer.

Let's begin with the more obvious *"Preventing Socialization Behavioral Issues"* that can lead to problems later in life, and proceed further into areas of *"Accidental Rewards"* that may not be so obvious, then touch upon *"Basic Rules and Boundaries"* and *"Adolescent Craziness"*, and finish this chapter with *"Less Obvious Stupid Human Mistakes"*.

Preventing Socialization Behavioral Issues

In order to prevent behavioral issues you first need to be aware of how easy it is to inadvertently create them yourself.

Much of how your Beagle learns to behave will depend entirely upon you, how extensively they were socialized as a puppy and how much they are continually being socialized throughout their life. Without proper socialization, even the most naturally friendly dog can become neurotic, unsociable and learn to act out aggressively toward unknown dogs, smaller animals or people. This is a situation that can get a sturdy dog, like the Beagle, deemed unfriendly or dangerous should they act out aggressively for any reason.

Many people don't realize how important it is to properly and continually socialize their dogs, in several different areas, because without proper socialization, many behavioral problems could become a daily occurrence.

Never make the mistake of thinking that you only need to socialize your Beagle puppy during the first few months of their life and that they will

Chapter 10: Humans Make a LOT of Stupid Mistakes

then be fine for the rest of their life, because all dogs require constant socializing.

As well, once they reach adolescence, their personality can really begin to assert itself, and this is when, without constant and vigilant daily socializing and training, any aggressive or anti-social tendencies may begin to erupt.

Generally speaking, the majority of an adult dog's habits and behavioral traits will be formed between the ages of birth and one year of age. While it is even more important to introduce puppies to a wide variety of sight, sounds, smells and situations during the most formative period in their young life, which is usually their first 16 weeks, all dogs, no matter their age, need to be exposed to different people, dogs, places and unusual sights and sounds throughout their entire adult life.

Socializing With Unknown Dogs

Any dog, despite their natural personality, that is not regularly socialized may become shy, nervous or suspicious around unfamiliar or unusual dogs, people or circumstances, which could lead to nervous or fearful behavior, which can then lead to aggression.

Daily on-leash dog walks are great opportunities for your Beagle to see and possibly meet other dogs and different people, as well as practice proper behavior when out and about.

Remember to take it slowly and never put your dog in a situation where he or she feels uncomfortable or feels forced into being around other canines. Your dog should always be given the option to walk away, with lots of space.

When socializing a young puppy, remember to introduce him or her first to the *more calm and friendlier* of dogs, because introducing your pup to a dog that may be overly boisterous or not so friendly with other dogs may result in a negative experience. Negative experiences at a young age may later result in a fear of other dogs. I would suggest finding a local puppy class with around 8-10 other puppies, so that you can carefully supervise socializing and guided play.

Chapter 10: Humans Make a LOT of Stupid Mistakes

Socializing With Unknown People

Proper socialization also means taking your puppy (or dog) everywhere with you and introducing them to many different people of all ages, sizes and ethnicities, so they will learn what is normal and acceptable in their daily life.

Also important, will be getting your puppy or dog used to the noise and unpredictable actions of young children. You will want to closely supervise play, so that children are not accidentally being too rough or screaming in high-pitched voices, because this can be very frightening for a young puppy or dog that is unfamiliar with children.

Be especially careful when introducing your puppy to young children who may accidentally hurt your puppy, because you don't want your dog to become fearful of children as this could lead to aggression issues later on in life.

Environmental Socialization

It can be a BIG mistake not to take the time to introduce your Beagle puppy to a wide variety of different environments, because when they are not comfortable with different sights and sounds, this could cause them (and you) stress and trauma later in their adult life.

Be creative and take your puppy everywhere you can imagine when they are young, so that no matter where they travel, whether strolling along a noisy city sidewalk or beside a peaceful shoreline, they will be equally comfortable.

Do not make the mistake of only taking your puppy into areas where you live and will frequently travel, because they need to also be comfortable visiting areas you might not often visit, such as noisy construction sites, airports or a shopping area across town.

Your puppy needs to see all sorts of sights, sounds and situations so that they will not become fearful, should they need to travel with you outside of their immediate neighbourhood.

Chapter 10: Humans Make a LOT of Stupid Mistakes

Your Beagle will take their cues from you, which means that when you are calm and in control of every situation, they will learn to be the same because they will trust and calmly follow your lead.

For instance, take them to the airport where they can watch people and hear planes landing and taking off, or take them to a local park where they can see a baseball game, or for a stroll beside a schoolyard at recess time when noisy children are out playing, or to the local zoo or farm and let them get a close up look at horses, pigs and ducks.

Again, never think that socialization is something that only takes place when your Beagle is a young puppy, as proper socialization is on-going for your dog's entire life.

Fear of Loud Noises

Many dogs can show extreme fear of loud noises, such as fireworks, sirens, thunderstorms or home security alarms. We humans need to learn how to either prevent this trauma in the first place or learn how to appropriately respond to a dog that is afraid of loud noises.

When you take the time to desensitize your dog to these types of noises when they are very young, it will be much easier on them during stormy weather, holidays such as Halloween or New Year's, when fireworks are often a part of the festivities, when an ambulance or fire truck roars past with sirens wailing, or when your fire or security alarm is activated.

Desensitization Devices: there are several ways you can help to desensitize your Beagle, so that they are not fearful of high-pitched alarms, and loud, popping noises, including the following:

CDs: you can purchase CD's that are a collection of unusual sounds, such as vacuums or hoovers, airplanes, sirens, smoke alarms, fireworks, people clapping hands, screaming children, and more (or you can easily make your own), that you can play while working in your kitchen or relaxing in your living room or lounge.

When you play these sounds and pretend that everything is normal, the next time your puppy or dog hears these types of sounds elsewhere,

Chapter 10: Humans Make a LOT of Stupid Mistakes

they will not become upset or agitated because they have learned to ignore them.

Bubble Wrap: is also another simple way to desensitize a Beagle that is fearful of unexpected sounds. Show them the bubble wrap, pop a few of the cells and if they do not run away, give them a treat. You can start with the bubble wrap that has small, quieter cells, and then graduate them to the larger celled (louder) bubble wrap. You can also take things even farther by blowing up some small paper bags or balloons and loudly popping them in front of your dog, or taking them to the rifle range.

Thunder Shirts: some dogs will respond well to wearing a *"Thunder Shirt",* which is specifically designed to alleviate anxiety or trauma associated with loud rumbling, popping or banging noises. The idea behind the design of the Thunder Shirt is that the gentle pressure it creates is similar to a hug that, for some dogs, has a calming effect.

Relaxation Collars: there are basically two types of collars designed to help relax or calm an upset puppy or dog. One uses scent or calming pheromones, while the other uses species-specific music at appropriate decibel levels to calm a fearful or stressed dog.

TV or Radio: sometimes all that is required to calm a Beagle that is stressed by loud noises is to play your inside TV or Radio station with the sounds of relaxing music, louder than you might normally, to help disguise the exterior noise of fireworks or thunder.

Always be aware that some dogs literally lose their minds and do things that make no sense when they hear the loud popping or screeching noises of fireworks and various alarms and start trembling, running or trying to hide and you cannot communicate with them at all.

Make certain that your dog cannot harm itself trying to escape from these types of noises, and if possible, calmly hold them until they begin to relax.

For instance, my dog, Boris, used to try and escape through the drain in the bathtub (go figure), because loud popping noises literally caused him to lose his mind.

Chapter 10: Humans Make a LOT of Stupid Mistakes

Make sure that YOU are acting appropriately yourself, by not panicking or having weak, *"feeling sorry"* energy around an upset dog, because this will only make matters worse. When the person who is supposed to be your dog's support system is also feeling weak, your dog will have nowhere to turn. Instead, support them by pretending that nothing is wrong and if you must talk to them, do so in a calm, yet assertive voice.

Never underestimate the importance of taking the time to continually (not just when they are puppies) socialize and desensitize your Beagle puppy to all manner of sounds, because to do so will make everyone happier in the future and will be teaching them to be a calm and well-balanced member of your family in every situation.

Accidental Rewards

Many times, we humans are guilty of accidentally rewarding our puppies and dogs for engaging in types of behavior we are not happy with, and the following are some of the more obvious things we may be doing that are inadvertently rewarding, and thus encouraging, an unwanted behavior.

Aggression Rewards

Many people unknowingly get into the habit of accidentally rewarding their puppies or dogs for displaying nervousness, fear, barking, growling or lunging at another dog or person by picking them up, talking soothingly, or offering them a treat.

When you accidentally reward your Beagle when they are displaying unbalanced energy, this actually turns out to be a reward for them, and you will be teaching them to continue with this type of unwanted behavior.

As well, picking up a small dog or puppy when they are growling, barking or acting out inappropriately, again rewards them and places them in a top dog position where they literally have just gained the higher ground.

Chapter 10: Humans Make a LOT of Stupid Mistakes

A dog in the *"top dog"* position feels more confident and will usually then become more dominant than the person or dog they may have just growled at when they were at *"ground level"*.

Rather than accidentally rewarding your Beagle for displaying unwanted behavior, the correct action to take in such a situation is to gently correct your puppy or dog with firm yet calm energy (that is just a little stronger than the energy your dog is displaying) by distracting them with a *"no"*, or a quick sideways snap of the leash to get their attention back on you, so that they learn to let you deal with whatever situation has caused them to react badly.

If you allow a fearful, nervous or shy dog to deal with situations that unnerve them and cause them act out aggressively when they encounter unfamiliar circumstances, you will have created a problem that could escalate into something very serious.

The same is true of situations where a young puppy may feel the need to protect itself from a larger or older dog that may come charging in for a sniff or is acting confrontational. It's the human guardian's responsibility to protect their puppy, so that they do not feel that they must react with fear or aggression in order to protect him or herself or the human at the other end of the leash.

No matter the age or size of your Beagle puppy or dog, allowing them to display aggression or any sort of unwanted behavior toward another dog, animal or person is never a laughing matter and this type of behavior must be immediately curtailed.

Excitement Rewards

It's important to recognize that attention paid to an overly excited or out-of-control puppy or dog, even negative attention, is likely going to be rewarding for your fur friend. If your dog is not receiving enough of your attention, they will quickly learn to do whatever it takes to get the attention they desire.

Bottom line, when you engage with an out-of-control puppy or dog, you end up actually rewarding them for acting out in an unstable manner,

Chapter 10: Humans Make a LOT of Stupid Mistakes

and encouraging them to continue with more overly exuberant behavior you might not be very pleased about.

Be careful that you're not teaching your Beagle to act out with crazy energy every time they see you.

For instance, chasing after a puppy when they have taken something they are not supposed to have, picking them up when they are barking or showing aggression, pushing them off when they jump on you or other people, or yelling when they refuse to come when called, are all forms of attention that can actually be rewarding and cause more of the same behavior.

Instead, remain calm and assertive and be consistent with your training, so that your Beagle learns how to control their energy and play quietly and appropriately without jumping on everyone or engaging in barking or mouthy behavior.

Interaction Rewards

If your Beagle displays excited energy simply from being petted by you, or anyone else, you will need to teach yourself, your family and your friends to ignore your fur friend until he or she calms down. Otherwise, you will be inadvertently teaching your canine companion that the touch of humans means excitement, and this behavioral problem will continue to escalate.

For instance, when you continue to engage with your overly excited puppy or dog, you are actually rewarding them for out-of-control behavior and literally teaching them that when they see humans, you want them to display excited energy.

Too many people encourage their dog to be nuts, for instance, when they return home and greet their dog in a highly excited state. While it's nice to know that your dog is happy to see you, when you forget about being your dog's pack leader just a few times, this may be enough to send your dog the message that seeing humans means they must now display out-of-control excitement.

Instead, when you come home, greet your dog calmly and quietly, and if they are at all excited, do NOT touch or talk to them until they calm down. Otherwise, your dog will learn that humans are a source of excitement, and long, consistently vigilant work on your part (with help from your friends and family) will be the only way to reverse this unwanted behavior (that can be quite dangerous with sturdy dogs, such as the Beagle, if they are around small children or unstable adults).

Another thing to keep in mind is that children are often a source of high energy and excitement that can cause a puppy or dog to quickly become extremely wound up.

If you don't want to create an on-going behavioral problem, that could accidentally get someone injured, you will need to be very vigilant about NOT permitting young children to engage with an excited Beagle.

Important Basic Rules and Boundaries

You can prevent many future behavioral problems when you take the time to ensure that your Beagle learns basic rules and boundaries. All that's necessary for effectively teaching your puppy (or dog) these basics is a calm, consistent and firm approach, combined with your endless patience.

Basic rules and boundaries would include things such as:

- no dogs allowed in the kitchen when preparing food
- no begging at the human's dinner table
- humans through the door first
- no sleeping in the human bed
- no raiding the garbage can
- no helping yourself to *"tootsie rolls"* from the cat's litter box
- no chasing the neighbor's cat

Many puppies are ready to begin basic training at about 10 to 12 weeks of age, and some will be ready at 8 weeks. However, be careful not to

Chapter 10: Humans Make a LOT of Stupid Mistakes

overdo it when they are less than four months of age, as their attention span may be short.

With younger puppies, make your training sessions no more than 5 or 10 minutes, positive and pleasant with plenty of praise and/or treats, so that your puppy will be looking forward to their next session.

Also, begin to introduce hand signals that go along with the verbal commands so that once they learn both, you can remove the verbal commands in favor of just hand signals.

Consistently teach your puppy or dog the *All Important Three*, which is the "Come", "Sit" and "Stay" commands (more about this in Chapter 12: Training Basics For a Happy Beagle), and use them every day in every opportunity to help your young dog progress through their unpredictable adolescent period.

Adolescent Craziness

Too often, we humans become impatient and frustrated and give up on our dogs when they transition from being the cute, cuddly and mostly obedient little puppy they once were and become all kinds of craziness.

Instead of riding the adolescent storm, it is often during this confusing and trying adolescent stage of a dog's life that they end up behind bars when the humans who promised to love and protect them, abandon their once happy fur friend at the local SPCA or rescue facility.

With consistency, understanding, the right information, and endless patience and perseverance, you and your Beagle can emerge out the other side of this adolescent period with a much stronger bond.

Firstly, you need to know that not all dogs go through an intensely crazy adolescent period. Secondly, when you remain consistent with your socializing and training during this time, you can live through puppy adolescence and come out the other side a much more knowledgeable and patient guardian.

Chapter 10: Humans Make a LOT of Stupid Mistakes

Remember, you've already lived through potty training, teething, socializing and basic rules and boundaries with your young Beagle, and you need to feel proud of all your accomplishments and the leaps and bounds you and your puppy have accomplished together over the last several months.

If your adolescent dog is beginning to act out and push your buttons, rather than giving up on them, it's time to remain calm, consistent and persistent, and re-visit basic rules and boundaries, while keeping in mind that you will eventually be able to enjoy the happy rewards that all those months of diligent puppy training have brought to your relationship.

During adolescence, you may experience several changes in your dog's personality that you're not exactly pleased about. For instance, your young Beagle may:

- no longer be as friendly with strangers
- start to show their stubborn side
- start to chase birds, cats and small rodents
- dig up your back yard
- ignore you when called
- appear to have suddenly gone deaf
- raid the garbage can
- ignore the basic commands they've already learned
- start to relieve themselves inside again
- begin to mark territory
- dig or climb their way out of the yard

Welcome to the world of canine adolescence, where it appears that all your previous work was for naught and your puppy has turned into some sort of monster.

Don't panic, because every dog is different and your dog's adolescent period may go by without notice. However, being prepared for the worst will help you ride any impending storm and get you both safely

Chapter 10: Humans Make a LOT of Stupid Mistakes

out the other side where you can enjoy an even closer relationship than you previously had.

The adolescent phase may be very subtle for your puppy or on the other hand, it may be so dramatic that frustration with your fur friend is becoming a daily occurrence.

Also keep in mind that the Beagle is a highly specialized *"scent hound"* with a superior sense of smell that can often distract them and make it seem like your dog has suddenly gone deaf.

If frustration is getting the upper hand, rather than letting it get worse, consider the benefits of hiring a professional, who can provide insight and valuable assistance to help you through this stage of your puppy's development.

Less Obvious Stupid Human Mistakes

There are many less obvious mistakes we humans can inadvertently make with our dogs that can also lead to behavioral problems later in life, some of which include:

Sleeping in Your Bed: many people make the mistake of allowing a crying puppy to sleep with them in their bed, and while this may help to calm and comfort a new puppy, it will set a dangerous precedent that can result in behavioral problems later in their life.

As much as it may pull on your heart strings to hear your new puppy crying the first couple of nights in their kennel, a little tough love at the beginning will keep them safe while helping them to learn to both love and respect you as their leader.

Picking Them Up at the Wrong Time: never pick your Beagle puppy up if they display nervousness, fear or aggression (such as growling) toward an object, person or other pet, because this will be rewarding them for unbalanced behavior.

Instead, your puppy needs to be gently corrected by you, with firm and calm energy, so that they learn not to react with fear or aggression.

Chapter 10: Humans Make a LOT of Stupid Mistakes

Armpit Alligators: when your Beagle is a small size, be aware that many guardians get into the bad habit of carrying a small dog or puppy far too much.

Remember that they need to be on the ground and walking on their own, so that they do not become overly confident because a dog that is carried by their guardian is literally being placed in the *"top dog"* position.

While you won't be able to carry around this puppy for very long, be aware that humans who constantly carry small dogs or puppies, rather than allowing them to walk on their own, can often inadvertently create what I refer to as an *"armpit alligator"* situation.

Even dogs that are friendly and not naturally wary or suspicious of strangers, such as the Beagle, can learn to become intolerant if they don't receive adequate socialization, which means that it is always possible to allow them to become protective or possessive of *"their"* humans.

Playing Too Hard or Too Long: many humans play too hard or allow their children to play too long or too roughly with their puppy. You need to remember that your young puppy tires very easily and especially during the critical growing phases of their young life, they need their rest.

Hand Play: always discourage your Beagle puppy from chewing or biting your hands, or any part of your body for that matter.

Do not get into the habit of playing the *"hand"* game, where you rough up your puppy and slide them across the floor with your hands, because this will teach them that your hands are playthings and you will have to work hard to break this bad habit.

When your puppy is teething, they will naturally want to chew on everything within reach, and this will include you. As cute as you might think it is, this is not an acceptable behavior and you need to gently, but firmly, discourage the habit.

Chapter 10: Humans Make a LOT of Stupid Mistakes

A light flick with a finger on the end of your puppy nose, combined with a firm "NO" and removing the enticing fingers by making a fist when they are trying to bite human fingers, will discourage them from this activity.

Not Getting Used to Grooming: not taking the time to get your Beagle used to a regular grooming routine, including bathing, brushing, toenail clipping and teeth brushing, can lead to a lifetime of trauma for both human and dog every time these procedures must be performed.

Set aside a few minutes each day for your grooming routine.

NOTE: get your Beagle used to being up high on a table or countertop when you are grooming them. This way, when it comes time for a full grooming session or a visit to the vet's office, where they will be placed on an examination table, they will not be stressed because this will already be a familiar situation.

Free Feeding: means to keep food in your puppy's bowl 24/7, so that they can eat any time of the day or night, whenever they feel like it.

While free feeding a young puppy can be a good idea (especially with very small dogs) until they are about four or five months old, many guardians often get into the bad habit of allowing their adult dogs to continue to eat food any time they want, by leaving food out 24/7.

Getting into this type of habit can be a serious mistake, as your dog needs to know that you are absolutely in control of their food.

Treating Them Like Children: do not get into the bad habit of treating your dog like a small, furry human; even though they may try their best to please you and their doggy smarts could help them to succeed in most instances, not honoring them for the amazing dog they are will only cause them confusion that could lead to behavioral problems.

IMPORTANT: remember that the one thing your dog is the absolute BEST at, is **Being a Dog**.

Chapter 10: Humans Make a LOT of Stupid Mistakes

A well-balanced dog thrives on rules and boundaries, and when they understand that there is no question that you are their leader and they are your follower, they will live a contented, happy and stress-free life.

Distraction and Replacement: when your Beagle puppy tries to chew on your hand, foot, clothing, or anything else that is not fair game, you need to firmly and calmly tell them "No", and then distract them by replacing what they are not supposed to be chewing with something they are permitted to chew, such as an appropriate toy.

Make sure that you happily praise them every time they choose the toy to chew on. If your puppy persists in chewing on you, remove yourself from the equation by getting up and walking away. If they are really persistent, put them inside their kennel with a favorite chew toy until they calm down.

Always praise your puppy when they stop inappropriate behavior or replace inappropriate behavior with something that is acceptable to you, so that they begin to understand what they can and cannot do.

Flat Collar Nightmares

Many humans simply don't realize how important it is to choose the "right" kind of collar for their canine companion. Add this to the fact that there is an ever-increasing array of tempting colors and styles to choose from and it's very easy to get distracted from choosing what you really need for your dog.

What you really need in a collar is one that will also keep your Beagle safe and secure. While the flat collar may be fine for a calm dog that never pulls, leaps about or suddenly tries to do an about face and take off running in a different direction to chase that teasing squirrel, this is not a very safe reality.

Of course, while you will choose what you will for your dog, after 40 some years of working with dogs and experiencing possibly every type of terrifying, unexpected disaster while out walking a dog, the ONLY collar I feel absolutely confident using (because I know that the dog I'm in control of cannot wiggle out of it), is the "Martingale" collar.

Flat collars, unless you have them cinched up so tight that you're almost cutting off your dog's air supply, can be fairly easy for most dogs to get out of.

All dogs are amazing athletes, and even though you may have a firm grip on that leash, they can back away from you, wiggle, twist and contort themselves in a quick instant, flip their head and the collar is off – bye, bye doggy!

The Martingale Collar

There are several reasons why the Martingale dog collar is far superior to a flat collar:

- comfortable for your dog to wear
- safe because your dog cannot wiggle out of it
- best training collar

The Martingale collar looks much the same as a flat collar, with one very important difference – there is a triangular piece of chain in the middle of it. This chain is attached to the collar with two rings, with a third ring in the middle of the chain, which is where you attach your leash.

When there is no tension on the collar (from them pulling on the leash), the collar hangs loose and comfortable. However, when there IS tension on the collar, that little piece of chain tightens so that your dog cannot get out of their collar.

My dog has been wearing the same Martingale "training" collar for almost 14 years and will continue to do so, because this collar conveys important messages between my dog and myself.

That little piece of triangular chain makes a slight noise when you sharply tug it, and this sends a message to your dog that you want their attention on you. It's simply the best collar for teaching your dog to walk calmly by your side and to remind them that YOU are in charge.

Chapter 10: Humans Make a LOT of Stupid Mistakes

When buying a Martingale collar for your Beagle, take him or her with you because it needs to be the correct size to fit over the widest part of their head. Then, once you've got the right size for your dog, you need to pay strict attention to the <u>correct way to adjust</u> the collar for maximum effect and safety.

Adjusting the Martingale Collar: once you've placed the collar over your dog's head, you need to adjust the length so that when you attach the leash to the outside ring and pull it tight, when the two inside rings come together, there is still a gap between these two rings of approximately two human finger widths. You never want the two inside rings to touch.

You can now enjoy comfortable and safe walks with your Happy Beagle companion.

Flexi-Leash Fiasco

Personally, flexi, retractable or extendable dog leashes are high on my list of pet peeves, for several important reasons, because they:

- are dangerous for human and dog alike
- allow the dog to be in the wrong walking position
- allow the humans to forget their responsibilities
- are difficult to securely grip
- are an excuse for not properly training your dog
- can accidentally break

While many people believe that a retractable leash is a good way to allow their dogs more freedom to roam while still keeping them securely attached, the above reasons highlight why these leashes can be a very bad idea. See below for more details.

Injury to human and dog: these leashes are usually spring-loaded, many feet long (usually 26 feet or 7.9 meters), and thin cords wound up inside a cumbersome plastic compartment with a handle and a button to control how much of the leash is extended.

Chapter 10: Humans Make a LOT of Stupid Mistakes

As you can imagine, it's far more difficult to control a dog that is roaming about 20 or more feet away from you, than it would be if they were attached to a standard 4 to 6 foot leash.

If your Beagle gets used to having a 20-foot (6 meter) or more leeway, they will be busy sniffing interesting scents, and can quickly run out into traffic, be surprised by another dog rushing in, or get tangled up with a person and a dog, which can cause both injury to the dogs and people, or may cause a fight between the two dogs.

These leashes are also serious tripping hazards that can cause many injuries.

For instance, the daughter of one of my dog whispering clients broke her toe as a result of tripping over a flexi-leash, I have suffered painful "rope" burns several times, and once was hit in the head (ouch!) with the hard and heavy plastic handle as it snapped back when the person holding it lost their grip and dropped it.

In addition, every flexi or retractable leash is equipped with a brake to stop the unwinding of the cord at various lengths. If your dog is running and all of a sudden comes to the end of their freedom, unless you drop the handle, they will be forced to come to a very abrupt stop that can injure a dog's neck or spine.

Incorrect Walking Position: the ONLY place your dog should ever be when you're out walking is beside you, and when you allow them to freely roam 20 or more feet from wherever you are, besides being lax about teaching your dog the correct walking position, you are *"telling"* them that you are no longer in charge. A dog that believes they are in charge can get you BOTH into a lot of trouble.

Forgetting Your Human Responsibilities: when you're out walking with your Beagle, as their leader, you are responsible for everything they do, including picking up after them. A retractable leash allows your dog to literally be out of your sight. While we're busy chatting with a neighbor or checking your phone messages, who knows what sort of *"message"* your dog may be depositing in the neighbor's yard.

Chapter 10: Humans Make a LOT of Stupid Mistakes

You can be fined for not picking up after your dog, not to mention gaining yourself a bad reputation from your neighbors or other more responsible dog walkers.

Difficult to Securely Grip: the flexi leash has a large, cumbersome handle that is quite slippery and difficult to securely hold onto. If your Beagle suddenly lunges or changes direction, the chances of you losing your grip are quite high, and when that happens, the consequences can be dangerously grave.

Once dropped, your dog is now dragging a bouncing, loudly clattering handle, which can be very noisy on a sidewalk or hard surface.

This very thing has happened to me in a busy, high traffic area, when walking someone else's dog, and I can tell you from first-hand experience that this is a highly stressful and frightening situation I would not want to wish on anyone.

Unless your dog has been trained to remain calmly sitting while rifles are fired near their head, this flexi leash that seems to be chasing them can be a very scary experience that will cause most dogs to run.

When your dog is scared, they will run even faster, while you run after them adding to the chaos with your panic-stricken screams to stop before they get killed trying to cross a busy intersection. Not a good scene.

Poor Training: while many might believe they are giving their Beagle more freedom by using a retractable leash, they are actually missing out on properly training their dog to heel beside them and to respond appropriately to the all-important "come" or "recall" command.

The very nature of a flexi leash is such that the dog is often out in front of the person who is supposed to be in charge, and always *"pulling"*, which to an approaching dog can look like an aggressive stance, resulting in the other dog thinking he or she must retaliate with a defensive stance. All of this, as you can imagine, has the potential to result in a scuffle between dogs and humans.

Chapter 10: Humans Make a LOT of Stupid Mistakes

Accidental Breakage: there is a great deal of wear on a small diameter cord that is constantly unwinding and rewinding and you may not notice a worn area until it actually breaks. Then, you've got a potential runaway dog disaster to hopefully recover from, before the dog gets severely injured or killed by a vehicle, or finds his or herself in some other type of serious trouble.

Improve your training, have better control, make your life easier, avoid injuries, and ensure the safety and security of yourself and your furry best friend by choosing a Martingale collar and a standard 4-foot leash.

In a Nutshell

It cannot be emphasized strongly enough how important it is to properly socialize your Beagle puppy, and understand that we humans often unknowingly reward our dogs at the wrong time, which can actually cause behavioral issues later in life.

Re-visit this Chapter information and think about what other mistakes you may be inadvertently making, so that you can do your best to avoid simple mistakes we humans often are guilty of making with our dogs, that can lead to an unhappy Beagle that suffers from behavioral problems later in life.

Also, when training your puppy or dog, keep in mind that the type of leash and collar you choose can make a big difference.

Chapter 11: Happy Beagle Body Language

"My little dog – a heartbeat at my feet."
— Edith Wharton

We all know good communication is not just about the words we use. Our tone of voice, energy and our body language help to package up and deliver our meaning every day. While most people can effectively communicate their thoughts and feelings through words, we need to generally be reliant upon reading our dog's body language in order to know if they are happy or sad.

Because our dogs don't speak our language, the only way to truly comprehend and communicate with them is for us to understand and appreciate what they are telling us through their body and vocal language.

Often, gestures or actions that we assume mean one thing are actually the dog telling us the exact opposite, and determining what that wagging tail or barking really means can sometimes be the difference between a belly rub and a bite.

Chapter 11: Happy Beagle Body Language

How happy would you be if you could not communicate with your family at home? Would you develop behaviour issues over time? Of course you would, and the same is also true for your beloved dog.

They need you to understand what they are "telling you" and how they feel, in order to be a happy family member. For instance, learning to properly "read" your dog's intentions can easily prevent an unwanted encounter during a visit to the local park.

Therefore, taking the time to educate yourself about basic canine body language and paying attention to your Beagle's body language (including their face, posture, barking and tail position) is an important prerequisite for raising a content and well-behaved dog.

This Chapter will teach you exactly that – to understand the basics of what your furry friend is trying to "tell" you and how they feel, so that you can share a happy lifelong partnership together.

So, don't wait and read on.

What's With All the Wagging and Barking?

While a well-socialized Beagle may often happily wag their flag of a tail, it can be a mistake to automatically assume that if your dog is wagging their tail, they are happy and friendly.

What Does the Wag Mean?

When determining a dog's true intent or demeanor, it's important to take into consideration the complete dog posture, rather than just the tail, because it's entirely possible that a dog can be wagging his or her tail just before it decides to take an aggressive lunge toward you or your dog.

More important in determining the emotional state of most dogs is the height or positioning of their tail. For instance, a tail that is held parallel to your dog's back usually suggests that they are feeling relaxed, whereas if the tail is held stiffly vertical, this usually means that they may be feeling aggressive or dominant.

Chapter 11: Happy Beagle Body Language

Also keep in mind that certain dog tails are carried differently for different reasons. For instance, the Beagle tail is a high waving flag, especially when they have encountered an interesting scent.

A tail held much lower can mean that your dog is feeling stressed, afraid, submissive or unwell and if the tail is tucked underneath the dog's body, this is most often a sign that the dog is feeling highly stressed, fearful or threatened by another dog or person.

Paying attention to your dog's tail can help you to know when you need to step in and make some space between your dog and another, more dominant dog.

Of course, different breeds naturally carry their tails at different heights, (and some dogs don't have tails), so you will need to take this into consideration so that you get used to their particular body language signals.

As well, the speed at which the tail is moving will give you an idea of the mental state of your dog, because the speed of the wag usually indicates how excited a dog may be.

For instance, a slow, slightly swinging wag can often mean that a dog is tentative about greeting another dog, and this is more of a questioning type of wag, whereas a fast-moving tail held high can mean that your dog is about to challenge or threaten another less dominant dog.

Also, a stalking stance, where your dog has raised hackles (hair along the back), lowers their head and slowly creeps forward with an intense stare often happens just before a serious attack. There is also a similar-looking *"play"* stance, and without practice, you may have difficulty identifying the difference between the two.

As an example, I've been sworn at after politely letting a guardian of a larger dog, who was unaware (and didn't want to know) that their dog was stalking my smaller dog and about to do him harm, so be careful how you approach these situations.

What Does the Bark Mean?

Chapter 11: Happy Beagle Body Language

Of course, our dogs bark for a wide variety of reasons, and every dog is different, depending upon their natural breed tendencies and how they were raised. This section discusses some of the more common reasons why a Beagle might be barking.

Communication: since the very first dog, they have communicated over long distances by howling to one another and when in closer proximity, barking to warn off other dogs approaching what they consider to be their territory, or in excitement or happiness when greeting another member of the dog pack.

Now, our domesticated dogs have learned that barking for a wide variety of reasons, such as when alerting us to someone approaching the home, in anticipation of their favorite food, when they are afraid, frustrated or bored, or to let us know they want to play, is an effective way to get the attention of us humans because barking is a loud and difficult noise to ignore.

Danger: many dogs will bark to alert us to visitors or intruders, and we need to learn how to understand the difference between what our dogs perceive as danger and what is truly dangerous, or indeed how to teach our best friends the difference?

We want our dogs to tell us when there is real, imminent danger and in this case, should the danger involve an unwanted intruder, we want them to bark loudly to possibly scare this threat away.

When our dogs are barking for a reason we are not yet aware of, we need to calmly assess the situation rather than immediately becoming annoyed.

We also need to remember that a Beagle's sense of smell, hearing and sometimes eyesight is far more acute than our own, which means that we need to give them an opportunity to tell us if they just heard, saw or sensed something that they are worried or uncertain about.

Rather than ignoring our dogs (or yelling at them) when they are attempting to *"tell"* us that something is bothering them, even if we ourselves understand that the noise the dog just heard is only the

Chapter 11: Happy Beagle Body Language

neighbor's kids coming home from school or a postal delivery, we need to respond appropriately.

We need to <u>calmly</u> acknowledge our dog's concern by saying, *"OK, good dog,"* and then ask them to come to you. This way you have quietly and calmly let your dog know that the situation is nothing to be concerned about and you have asked them to move away from the target they are concerned about, which places you in control, and which will usually stop the barking.

On a Scent: the Beagle is a "scent hound" with a highly superior sense of smell, and many of them will start to yodel or howl as soon as an interesting scent reaches their nose.

Attention: many dogs will learn to bark to get their owner's attention, just because they are bored or want to be taken outside for an interesting walk or a trip to the local park to chase a ball.

Our canine companions are very good at manipulating us in this way, and if we fall for it, we are setting up an annoying precedent that could plague us for the remainder of our relationship.

For instance, I shared my life with a Blue Heeler who would go berserk with loud barking every time we drove near a park or when we arrived at a park. Even so, I would never reward him for barking, because as annoying and hard on the eardrums as it was, I had to sit calmly inside the vehicle until he stopped barking. If I had let him immediately bound out of the vehicle, I would have inadvertently taught my dog that barking got him exactly what he wanted.

When a dog is barking to gain their guardian's attention, for whatever reason, before we immediately capitulate, first we need to calmly ask our dog to do something for us. After our dog has performed a calm and quiet task for us, such as sit or lie down, then we can decide to give our dog our undivided attention on our terms.

Often you will see a dog and their guardian at the local dog park playing fetch and when the human is not throwing that ball quickly enough to satisfy the dog's desire to run and fetch, the dog will be

Chapter 11: Happy Beagle Body Language

madly barking at the guardian. This is the equivalent of being sworn at in doggy language.

Don't make the mistake of allowing your Beagle to manipulate you in this situation, because if you do, you will soon create a bad habit that will very quickly become not just annoying to you, but also annoying to everyone else at the park.

Before throwing a ball or Frisbee for a Beagle that loves to retrieve, it's important to always ask the dog to sit and make eye contact with you.

Often the types of canines that are overly exuberant with chasing a ball or Frisbee have learned this barking behavior from their humans, who allowed themselves to be literally at the beck and call of their dog, and created this irritating habit by throwing the ball every time the dog barked.

In this situation, if you allow your dog to dictate to you when you will throw the ball, they will quickly learn that barking gets them their desired result, and you have just created an annoying, rude dog who is yelling at you in doggy language to do their bidding.

In this type of ball-retrieving scenario, the dog has become ball *"obsessed"* and is no longer really paying attention to the guardian's commands, as they are solely focusing on where the ball is.

While there are many situations in which your Beagle may howl or yodel to convey that they've discovered an interesting scent, in all other situations where the barking is done to demand attention, a toy, an object or food, this is when you need to ask them to do something for you, and then only if you want to give them what they are asking for, do you follow through.

As an example, I once had a client whose Beagle would start to whine and bark every time she stopped to talk with a neighbor. This was big time annoying to everyone, not to mention being almost impossible to carry on a conversation. A little dog-whispering session fixed the problem that had been actually created by the guardian, who had permitted her dog to be the center of attention at all times, and the

Chapter 11: Happy Beagle Body Language

barking and whining was how her dog had learned to return his guardian's attention back to him.

Bottom line, remember to stay calm when your cute puppy is demanding attention, because even negative attention can be rewarding for your dog, and can lead down a future, unwanted path where he or she will learn further habits that will not be particularly endearing for the human side of the relationship when the cute puppy has become an adult.

Boredom or Separation Anxiety: many Beagles, especially those who have not been properly trained or that have not been allowed to understand that they have rules and boundaries, and are treated like children, will bark and loudly yodel when left at home and are bored or are feeling the anxiety of being alone.

Many times, we humans believe that our dog is barking when being left alone, because he is experiencing *"separation anxiety"*, when in fact what the dog is really experiencing is the frustration of observing a member of the pack which they believe to be their follower (i.e. You) leaving them.

This can happen when you are not a strong enough leader for your Beagle and they have taken over. They may then loudly verbalize their frustration and displeasure because, in the dog world, the pack follower (which you have allowed yourself to be) does NOT leave the pack leader (them). *I've seen this type of situation many times over, and once the human side of the relationship steps up and takes control, it quickly reverses.*

Breaking your dog of the habit of loud barking when they are left alone can be solved in different ways, with the most obvious being that you simply take your dog with you wherever you go, because after all, they are pack animals, and in order for them to be really happy and well balanced, they need the constant direction of their leader (which is supposed to be you).

Another much more lengthy and time consuming way to solve a barking problem, could involve hiring a professional to help assess why

Chapter 11: Happy Beagle Body Language

the problem has occurred in the first place and then devise an effective plan to reverse the problem that will work for each unique situation.

Fear or Pain: another reason your Beagle will bark is when they are very frightened or in pain and this is usually a type of bark that sounds quite different from all the others, often being a combination of a bark and a whine, or a yelping type of noise.

This is a bark that you will want to pay close attention to, so that you can quickly respond and offer the assistance that your puppy or dog may need.

Whatever reason your dog may be barking for, always remember that this is how they communicate and *"tell"* us that they want something or are concerned, afraid, nervous or unhappy about something, and as their guardians, we humans need to pay attention.

Raised Hackles: when your Beagle approaches with raised hackles (the hair along the dog's back), while this can be an indication that the dog may be approaching with dominant or aggressive tendencies, it also may be an indication that he is excited, fearful, startled, anxious or lacks confidence.

In any of these circumstances, it's a good idea to be respectful and keep your distance until you can assess what's really going on, because even a reactive, fearful dog can quickly turn into a biting dog, and I can tell you from personal experience that being bitten by any dog really hurts.

In a Nutshell

Learning your Beagle's particular body language can take some time, and this Chapter will help you get started. The more you are out and about with your dog, visiting and socializing in local parks and going on walks where you will find other dogs, animals and people to observe, the more opportunity you will have to become skilled at recognizing the many subtleties of dog body language.

Paying attention to your Beagle's verbal and body-language signals as explained above, will help you figure out what message they are trying to get across to you and this can make all the difference in preventing frustration for you both while raising a happy and well-behaved dog.

One last thought about body language and energy – check in with yourself before you walk out the door with your dog, because if you're not in the moment and have your mind on something that has nothing to do with having a successful and pleasant walk with your dog, you may be setting yourself up for trouble.

If you go out the door with your dog while displaying sad, weak or confusing energy, your Beagle will pick up on this, and your energy can literally be the cause of, for instance, an uncomfortable encounter with another person walking their dog.

It's very important to keep in mind that when walking with a dog, if they sense that you are not completely in control, they will take this unspoken "cue" from you that being in charge has now defaulted to him or her.

You <u>never</u> want any dog to feel they must protect you from the postman, neighbor's cat or that cute little Chihuahua walking across the street, because if they do, you're literally out walking with a highly unpredictable, live "weapon" that could decide to go off at any moment.

While most Beagles are pleasant with other dogs and friendly with people, if they have been properly socialized and trained, should you permit them to get out of control, you could end up with a lawsuit on your hands, and/or sky-high veterinary bills, and that's if you're lucky. However, if your dog harms another dog, animal or person, the consequences could be far worse, even resulting in a death sentence for your loyal companion, or a ruling that your dog cannot be seen in public unless they are wearing a muzzle.

Chapter 12: Training Basics for a Happy Beagle

*"When your children are teenagers,
it's important to have a dog so that
someone in the house is happy to see you."*
— Nora Ephron

It's no surprise that a properly trained Beagle will be a much happier, safe and more secure companion that everyone enjoys being around, and that will be far less likely to develop behaviour issues later in life.

When your dog respects your leadership and there is no question that YOU are in charge, they can then relax and let you take the lead on training them, which is as it should be. Developing a basic training program and learning to teach your Beagle commands and discipline is all part of starting your dog off on the right paw.

Therefore, this Chapter will focus on training basics and tips, including hand signals, as well as simple tricks that your Beagle will love to learn. Take heed humans, because you will be very happy you spent the time to learn everything contained in these pages.

Chapter 12: Training Basics for a Happy Beagle

All of our canine companions are amazing, natural athletes and because of this, no matter their size or breed, they need daily exercise to stay fit and healthy, so that they can be happily well-mannered, and part of their exercise routine includes learning at least three very important training basics, which are "Come – Sit – Stay".

Every dog will require daily exercise to stay happy and healthy. They will love going for hikes, walks and little adventures with you. Your Beagle may especially enjoy learning routines and fun canine sports with their guardian as well as playing and socializing in a pack of other dogs.

Any type of disciplined exercise you can engage in with your dog will help to exercise both their body and their mind and will burn off pent-up daily energy reserves, so that your dog will be a happy and contented companion that is relaxed and not overweight.

If you find that your Beagle is being a pest by chewing inappropriate items around the home or being demanding of your time, or especially unruly when visitors come to call, this is likely because their mind is not being challenged enough or their body is not being exercised often enough, or long enough each day to drain out their daily pent-up energy reserves.

A healthy, adult Beagle will thrive when being walked several times each day and may also enjoy the challenge of being engaged in other forms of disciplined canine activity, such as Agility or Nose Work.

The loyal, friendly and willing to learn Beagle is a strongly built breed of small companion dog that despite their stubborn streak and stout build is able to excel in many canine sports and bring home those blue ribbons in the sporting, obedience and show arenas.

Use your imagination and find out what canine sports your dog may enjoy learning. So long as you prove to him or her that you mean what you say through firm direction and consistency, rather than too many treats, they will not feel the need to manipulate or question your authority, and will happily follow your direction.

Chapter 12: Training Basics for a Happy Beagle

The Beagle can seem to be stubborn, and often this is simply their superior sense of smell distracting them from the situation at hand. They will need fair, firm guidance and discipline from a young age, which includes rules and boundaries, so that they understand you are the boss, and are acutely aware of the line they cannot ever cross, and depending on the particular dog, this should be easily attainable even for a novice guardian.

Even at the young age of eight to ten weeks, most dogs are capable of beginning to learn anything you can teach. If you wait until they are six months old before beginning any serious training program, you could already have a stubborn problem on your hands and a young and strong little dog that may be unwilling to heed your commands.

The backbone of helping to develop a well-balanced and happy Beagle is to provide them with a routine that ensures sufficient time to satisfy their particular physical and mental exercise needs, in combination with additional time to play, sniff, search and explore their world every day.

What you can teach this energetic canine depends entirely upon you and the time and patience you have to devote to their education. No matter what you decide to teach your dog, always train with patience, kindness and positive rewards.

All training sessions should be happy and fun-filled with plenty of food rewards and positive reinforcement, which will ensure that your dog is a happy, attentive student who trusts and respects you as their leader and looks forward to learning new commands, tricks and routines.

Beagle Puppy Training Basics

First, choose a "Discipline Sound" that will be the same for every human family member. This will make it much easier for your Beagle puppy to learn what they can or cannot do and will be very useful when warning or redirecting your puppy before they engage in unwanted behavior.

Chapter 12: Training Basics for a Happy Beagle

The best types of sounds are short and sharp, so that you and your family members can quickly say them and so that the sound will immediately get the attention of your puppy, as you want to be able to easily interrupt them when they are about to make a mistake.

It doesn't really matter what the sound is, so long as it gets your dog's attention and everyone in the family is consistent. A sound that is very effective in most cases is a simple *"UH!"* sound that is said sharply and with emphasis.

Most puppies and dogs respond immediately to this sound and if caught in the middle of doing something they are not supposed to be doing, they will quickly stop and give you their attention or back away from what they were doing.

Next, your puppy needs to learn the Three Most Important Words, which are *"Come"*, *"Sit"* and *"Stay"*. These three basic commands will ensure that your puppy remains safe in almost every circumstance.

For instance, when your puppy correctly learns the *"Come"* command, you can always quickly bring them back to your side if you should see danger approaching. Also, when you teach your puppy the *"Sit"* and *"Stay"* commands, you will be further establishing your leadership role, and a puppy that understands that their human guardian is their leader will be a safe and happy follower.

Most puppies are ready to begin training at approximately 10 to 12 weeks of age (and some even earlier), so make your training sessions no more than 5 or 10 minutes (2 or 3 times a day), positive and pleasant with lots of praise and/or treats so that your puppy will be looking forward to their next session.

Come: while most Beagle puppies will be capable of learning commands and tricks at quite a young age, the first and most important command you need to teach your puppy is the recall, or *"Come"* command.

Begin the *"Come"* command inside your home. Go into a larger room, such as your living room area. Place your puppy in front of you and

Chapter 12: Training Basics for a Happy Beagle

attach their leash or a longer line to their Martingale collar, while you back away from them a few feet.

Say the command *"Come"* in an excited, happy voice and hold your arms open wide. If they do not immediately come to you, gently give a tug on the leash, so that they understand that they are supposed to move toward you. When they come to you, happily praise them and give a treat they really enjoy.

Once your puppy can accomplish a *"Come"* command almost every time inside your home, you can then graduate them to a nearby park or quiet outside area where you will repeat the process and where there are many more distractions. In order to keep yourself and your Beagle safe, he or she needs to always come to you when asked, despite whatever distractions may be nearby.

You may want to purchase an extra-long, lightweight line (25 or 50 feet), so that you are always attached to your puppy and can encourage them in the right direction should they become distracted by noises, scents and other dogs. Try to choose a time of day when there will be fewer distractions while you are training.

Keep in mind that even after teaching your Beagle the *"Come"* command, their nose will always take precedence over the commands you are teaching. This means that even when they are really good at the recall command, if an interesting scent distracts them, they may ignore you. Always keep this dog on leash when working in an area where they can easily run off in pursuit of an intriguing scent.

Sit: the "Sit" and *"Stay"* commands are both easy commands to teach that will help to keep your puppy safe and out of danger in almost every circumstance. Find a quiet time to teach these commands when your puppy is not overly tired.

Ask your puppy to "Sit" and if they do not yet understand the command, show them what you mean by gently squeezing with your thumb and middle finger the area across the back that joins with their back legs.

Chapter 12: Training Basics for a Happy Beagle

Do NOT just push them down into a sit, as this can cause damage to their back or joints. When they sit, give them a treat and praise them.

When you say the word "*Sit*", at the same time show them the hand signal for this command. While you can use any hand signal, the universal hand signal for *"Sit"* is right arm (palm open facing upward) parallel to the floor, and then raising your arm while bending at the elbow toward your right shoulder. Once your dog is sitting reliably for you, remove the verbal "Sit" and replace it with the hand signal.

Every time you take your dog out for a walk, which is often a cause of excitement, get into the habit of asking them to sit quietly and patiently at every stage of your walk.

For instance, ask your Beagle to sit and patiently wait while you put on their leash, while you put on your shoes or jacket, after you approach the door, after you are on the other side of the door, while you lock the door, every time you arrive at a street intersection or crosswalk, every time you stop during your walk to speak to a neighbor, greet a friend or admire the view, etc., and do this all in reverse when heading back home.

When you persist with the *"Sit"* training, it will soon become automatic for your dog to calmly sit every time you stop walking. When you ask your dog to sit for you, they are learning several things all at once; that they must remain calm while paying attention to you, that you are the boss, that they must look to you for direction and that they must respect you as their leader.

Keep in mind that a sitting Beagle puppy is much easier to control than one standing at the alert, ready to bolt out the door or jump on someone. As well, because the action of sitting helps to calm the mind of an excited puppy (or dog), teaching your puppy the *"Sit"* command is a very important part of their daily interactions with your family members as well as people you may meet when out on a walk.

When you ask your puppy to *"Sit"* before you interact in any way with them, before you go out, before you feed them, etc., you are helping to quiet their mind, while teaching them to look to you for direction, and

Chapter 12: Training Basics for a Happy Beagle

at the same time making it more difficult for them to jump, lunge or disappear out a door.

Stay: once your puppy can reliably "Sit", say the word *"Stay"* (with authority in your voice) and hold your outstretched arm, palm open toward their head while backing away a few steps. If they try to follow, calmly say "No" and put them back into *"Sit"*. Give a treat and then say again, *"Stay"* with the hand signal and back away a few steps.

Practice these three basic *"Come", "Sit", "Stay"* commands everywhere you go, and use the *"Sit"* command as much as you can to ensure its success rate.

As your puppy gets older, and their attention span increases, you will be able to train for longer periods of time and introduce more complicated routines.

Hand Signals

It's really important to use the hand signals that go along with the verbal commands during training, so that once your Beagle learns both, you can remove the verbal commands in favor of just hand signals.

Hand signal training is by far the most useful and efficient training method for your Beagle. All too often we inundate our canine companions with a great deal of chatter and noise that they really don't understand, but because they are so willing to be part of our world, they soon learn the meaning of many words.

Contrary to what some people might think, the first language of a Beagle (or any dog) is a combination of sensing energy and watching body language, which requires no spoken word or sound.

Therefore, when we humans take the time to teach our dog hand signals for all their basic commands, we are communicating with them at a level they instinctively understand, plus we are helping them to become a focused follower, as they must watch us in order to understand what is required of them.

Chapter 12: Training Basics for a Happy Beagle

Simple Tricks

When teaching your dog tricks, in order to give him or her extra incentive, find a treat that they really like and give the treat as a positive reward, which will help solidify a good performance.

Most dogs will be extra attentive during training sessions when they know that they will be rewarded with their favorite treats – especially this dog, who will usually have a healthy appetite.

If your puppy is less than six months old when you begin teaching them tricks, keep your training sessions short (no more than 5 or 10 minutes) and fun. As they become adults, you can extend your sessions, as they will be able to maintain their focus for longer periods of time.

Shake a Paw: who doesn't love a well-trained dog that knows how to shake a paw? This is one of the easiest tricks to teach your dog.

TIP: most dogs are naturally either right or left pawed. If you know which paw your dog favors, ask them to shake this paw. Find a quiet place to practice, without noisy distractions or other pets, and stand or sit in front of your dog. Place them in the sitting position and have a treat in your left hand.

Say the command *"Shake"* while putting your right hand behind their left or right paw and pulling the paw gently toward yourself until you are holding their paw in your hand. Immediately praise them and give them their favorite treat.

Most Beagles will learn the "Shake" trick quite quickly, and very soon, once you put out your hand, your dog will immediately lift their paw and put it into your hand, without your assistance or any verbal cue.

Practice every day until they are 100% reliable with this trick, and then it will be time to add another trick to their repertoire.

Roll Over: you will find that just as your dog is naturally either right or left pawed, they will also naturally want to roll either to the right or the left side. Take advantage of this by asking your dog to roll to the side they naturally prefer.

Chapter 12: Training Basics for a Happy Beagle

Sit with your Beagle on the floor and put them in a lie down position. Hold a treat in your hand and place it close to their nose without allowing them to grab it. While they are in the lying position, move the treat to the right or left side of their head (the nose will follow the treat), so that they have to roll over to get to it.

You will very quickly see which side they want to naturally roll to, and once you see this, move the treat to this side. When they roll over to this side, immediately give them the treat and praise them.

You can say the verbal cue *"Over"* while you demonstrate the hand signal motion (moving your right hand in a circular motion) or moving the treat from one side of their head to the other with a half circle motion.

Sit Pretty: while this trick is a little more complicated, and most dogs pick up on it very quickly, remember that every dog is different so always exercise patience.

Find a quiet space with few distractions and sit or stand in front of your dog and ask them to *"Sit"*. Have a treat nearby (on a countertop or table) and when they sit, use both of your hands to lift up their front paws into the sitting pretty position, while saying the command *"Sit Pretty"*. Help them balance in this position, while you praise them and give them the treat.

Once your Beagle can perform the balancing part of the trick quite easily without your help, sit or stand in front of your dog while asking them to *"Sit Pretty"*. Holding the treat above their head at the level of their nose would be when they sit pretty.

If they attempt to stand on their back legs to get the treat, you may be holding the treat too high, which will encourage them to stand on their back legs to reach it. Go back to the first step and put them back into the *"Sit"* position and again lift their paws while their backside remains on the floor.

Sit Pretty hand signal: hold your straight arm, fully extended, over your dog's head with a closed fist.

Make this a fun and entertaining time for both of you and practice a few times every day until they can *"Sit Pretty"* on hand signal command every time you ask.

A smart young puppy should be able to easily learn these basic tricks before they are six months old and when you are patient and make your training sessions short and fun for your dog, they will be eager to learn so much more.

Adult Training

The Beagle will thrive when involved in different training routines and/or canine sports. Therefore, in order to ensure a happy and healthy dog that will not develop behaviour issues out of boredom or laziness, make sure that you get your Beagle involved in as much activity as possible, including advanced Obedience, Agility or Nose Work.

When your dog is a full-grown adult (approximately two years of age), you will definitely want to begin more complicated or advanced training sessions.

When you have the desire and patience, you may be surprised at how many commands, tricks, routines or canine sports you can teach a happy, willing Beagle who trusts and respect their human guardian.

For instance, you may wish to teach your adult dog more advanced tricks, such as freestyle dance, or the opposite sided paw shakes or rollovers, which are more difficult than you might expect.

If you and your dog are really enjoying learning new tricks or routines together, consider teaching them a series of hand signals, such as *"Commando crawl"*, *"Speak"* or *"Jump through the human hoop"*, or perhaps get them involved in an organized canine sport.

Teaching your dog tricks and routines builds trust and respect, is fun for both of you, and a healthy way to exercise both your dog's mind and body, which will result in a happy, contented and well-behaved companion.

Chapter 12: Training Basics for a Happy Beagle

Over-Exercising

Be especially careful about over-exercising your dog when really young, because their muscles and bones are not yet fully developed, and especially on hot days (carry water for them), because like humans, dogs can also collapse from heat stroke.

Playtime

Every dog needs some down time or regular playtime each day, and while every dog will be different with respect to what types of games they may enjoy, most Beagles will really love any game involving retrieving a ball or finding a scent.

The Beagle may also be a very excited participant in a fun game of *"Search"*, where you ask your dog to *"Sit/Stay"* while you hide a favorite treat that they then have to use their nose to find. To begin teaching the "Search" game, first time ask your dog to sit/stay while you slowly back away and place a treat where they can actually still see it. Return to where they are in their sit/stay and say, "OK! Search!" and point to where you just placed the treat. Each time you play this game, you can place the treat farther and farther away and completely out of their sight before you release them to "Search!"

After a disciplined walk with your dog, they will also enjoy being given the opportunity for some off-leash freedom to really stretch out by running free to play and socialize with other similar-sized dogs at the local dog park.

In a Nutshell

Taking the time to teach your dog basic rules and boundaries, plus simple tricks, will keep them both mentally and physically healthy and happy and you will raise a well-behaved dog that is a joy to be around.

The Beagle has great stamina, and requires more daily exercise than many other breeds. This means that in order to ensure a healthy, happy and contented dog that is not overweight and will not develop behavior issues out of boredom or neglect, you must take the time to involve

Chapter 12: Training Basics for a Happy Beagle

them in daily vigorous exercise; that can include different activities, such as running or hiking at your side, jogging beside your bicycle or canine sports where they get to use their superior sense of smell.

Chapter 13: What If You Slip Up?

"Everything I know, I learned from dogs."
— Nora Roberts

All the information, suggestions, tips and advice given in this book is the result of more than 40 years experience helping humans positively and effectively interact with the canine world.

If you take all that is written on these pages to heart, and regularly and consistently apply them, your Beagle will grow up to be a happy family member that will not have to suffer from any behavioral issues.

However, if your lifestyle drastically changes, you forget to exercise your dog, keep on top of basic or advanced training, or you slip up for any number of reasons, problems may inevitably occur.

For instance, you may end up becoming too busy or distracted with your human life to provide your canine companion with what he or she needs on a daily basis to be a happy and fulfilled member of your family.

Realistically, there may be any number of other reasons why you don't consistently apply the information given here, and the following is an

Chapter 13: What If You Slip Up?

outline of just a few of the more common behavioral issues that may occur, with some tips that may help you get back on track.

When reading the following pages, please keep in mind that a specific behavioral problem is usually the result of many different possibilities or circumstances that have taken place between the human individual or family and the particular dog.

This means that properly addressing a specific unwanted behavior often needs the assistance of a professional with a personal approach, who can ask the right questions to determine how the unwanted behavior occurred, because it's often not what you may have initially thought.

Therefore, to generically outline possible ways to reverse an unwanted behavior will be a guessing game, because without knowing the circumstances of the guardian and their family, and understanding the situation that triggered the unwanted behavior, I can only make my best guess based on previous experience with similar problems.

As an example, there might be many reasons why the Beagle in question is chewing the tassels on your Persian rug. For instance, this could be because they:

- are hungry
- are teething
- have a taste for wool
- think the tassels are a toy
- are a super high energy dog
- are left alone and are bored
- haven't been given appropriate toys to chew
- have not been taught rules and what is appropriate
- need a guardian with stronger leadership energy
- are under-exercised
- are over-stimulated

As you can see, it's possible for almost endless scenarios and reasons why a dog may develop a particular behavioral issue.

Chapter 13: What If You Slip Up?

Therefore, please understand that without close observation and much more information explaining a particular situation, the following few common behavioral problems and the suggestions for alleviating them, will be my best guess.

Chewing Inappropriate Items
[Re-visit *"Distraction and Replacement"* in Chapter 10]

If your Beagle puppy or dog is chewing the carpet, your fingers, the legs of the coffee table, or any other inappropriate item(s) that are not dog toys, rather than getting upset with your dog, you need to train yourself to be much more vigilant, and then distract and replace.

First make sure that all the chewing is not just because the puppy is teething. Have compassion because teething is painful for the puppy and they must chew to help alleviate the pain while those adult teeth are growing in.

Always make sure your puppy has plenty of chew toys and to help with the teething pain, give your puppy an old T-towel soaked in water, tied in knots and frozen in the freezer as a chew toy.

If your Beagle is a little older, already has pushed through their adult set of teeth and has decided, for instance, that the legs on your coffee table are good chew toys, it is possible that you:

- are not paying attention and taking the time to make sure your dog receives enough daily exercise, and/or,
- are not teaching your dog what is, and what is not, appropriate for chewing by saying a firm and convincing **"No"**, replacing the table leg with a toy they are allowed to chew, and praising them when they've got the right thing between their teeth.

Being Fearful of Loud Noises
[Re-visit *"Fear of Loud Noises"* in Chapter 10]

If you have raised a Beagle that has a fear of loud, popping noises, you have not taken the time to read this information and apply the suggestions outlined, so read it now and practice until your dog loses or at least diminishes their fear.

Chapter 13: What If You Slip Up?

Excessive Excitement When Friends Visit
[Re-visit *"Chapter 3: Overview of the Happy Beagle"* and *"Chapter 12: Training Basics for a Happy Beagle"*]

Make sure that you begin to teach an excitable young Beagle to be a calm follower as soon as you bring him or her home.

Always ignore an excited dog and do not touch them until they are calm and relaxed, otherwise you will inadvertently teach them that it is acceptable behavior for them to be excited every time they see a human.

If they are overly excited when friends come to visit, stand between your dog and your friends, and create some space by pointing away and firmly telling your dog, *"GO"*, and also ask your friends to ignore him or her.

Also, if you've been properly training your puppy or dog, you will have taught them to *"Sit"* on command, and a sitting dog is much more relaxed and easier to control.

Acting Aggressively on a Walk
[Re-visit *"Chapter 12: Training Basics for a Happy Beagle"*]

Make sure that your Beagle is walking at your side without pulling on the leash when you are out for a walk.

When you train your dog to walk beside you, this "tells" them that YOU are their leader and in charge of every situation, which means they will be much less likely to act out or attempt to "protect" you from outside stimuli. If they DO try, immediately give a sharp snap on that Martingale collar along with a strong *"NO!"* to remind them who is the boss.

Pulling When on Leash
[Re-visit *"The Martingale Collar"* in Chapter 10]

If your dog is pulling on leash, chances are high that he or she is not wearing the proper training collar and you have not taken the time to teach them to quietly walk at your side.

Chapter 13: What If You Slip Up?

Buy your dog a Martingale collar, properly adjust it, and then the next time they try to pull ahead of you, give a sharp snap to this collar (toward yourself) and firmly say the word "*Heel*".

Repeating this process until your Beagle understands can take a few minutes or even several days, as each dog is different – be consistent and persistent until your dog gets it.

Also, turning circles and changing directions suddenly when on a leash walk will quickly help to teach your dog their proper walking position, because if they are ahead of you they are going to be stepped on or walked into.

Stealing Food or Raiding the Garbage Can
[Re-visit "*Ideal Living Conditions for a Happy Beagle*" in Chapter 6]

Make sure you absolutely understand that the Beagle usually has a strong appetite. Keep in mind that, if given the opportunity, some dogs will literally eat themselves to death, or will eat food that is toxic to their physiology. This means that in order to avoid this possibility, you must be a vigilant guardian and make sure that you never leave any food unattended or where they can reach it.

Not Obeying Commands
[Re-visit "*Chapter 12: Training Basics for a Happy Beagle*"]

A well-trained Beagle is one that obeys the basic "*Come/Sit/Stay*" commands. If your dog is not obeying your commands, you have not taken the time to properly train them, or you are too weak a leader, with the result being that he or she will take a stubborn attitude, they will ignore you and they will not respect you as their leader. Get to work right away, step up your energy to ensure you are a strong enough leader, and train your dog so that everyone will be happy.

We all have our off days, so don't get down on yourself if you occasionally slip up and are not being as vigilant, strong and confident a leader as you need to be with this dog's basic and/or advanced training and daily maintaining of rules and boundaries.

Chapter 13: What If You Slip Up?

In a Nutshell

We humans will always have days when we are not as vigilant as we need to be, which means that we will inevitably "slip up" sometimes when raising our fur friends.

What you need to remember is that it's not the end of the world, because there is always a solution, and often simply re-reading the relevant chapters in this book can quickly and easily get you back on track to raising a happy and well-behaved Beagle that is a pleasure to be around.

Chapter 14: Surprise Bonus Chapter

*"A well-trained dog will make no attempt
to share your lunch. He'll just make you feel
so guilty that you can't enjoy it."*
— Helen Thomson

If you thought that you had reached the end of this book, well surprise, not quite yet, as I'd like to leave you with some canine wisdom and a couple of funny, true stories.

The following Question and Answer (Q&A) section is written from the dog's perspective, and although you may find it amusing, there are also valuable human lessons to be learned, if anyone is paying attention.

First, let me set the scene for the following situations:

This is a young, busy family, consisting of Mom and Dad, who work at home, one 12-year-old girl, and one 14-year-old boy, who share their lives with a sweet, friendly, neutered, 1-year-old Beagle named *Barney*. They all live together in a large house with a medium-sized, fenced yard and a vegetable garden out the back.

Chapter 14: Surprise Bonus Chapter

The following questions, asked by various members of the family, are directed to the dog and answered by the dog, as if the dog could talk like their humans.

Each question that the Beagle answers is followed by a short synopsis of the *"lesson"* we humans can learn from these various interactions.

Mom: **"Oh No, Barney! Why did you pee on the floor?"**

Barney: *"I just couldn't hold it any longer after that big drink. Please don't be mad at me."*

Lesson: Humans often lead very busy lives, and in order to ensure their dog remains happy, they still need to always pay attention and put their canine friend's habits and needs ahead of their own. Nobody was paying attention or noticing that this young dog had a big drink over an hour ago. It's not the dog's fault he couldn't hold it any longer – he should have been taken out before this accident happened.

Girl: **"Yuckeeee! Barney, what is that? Did you puke on the floor?"**

Barney: *"I found half a box of crackers in the boy's room, and it looked like he left it for me, so I ate what was left. I think it was too salty."*

Lesson: Dogs will eat anything even remotely smelling of food, and some dogs have sensitive stomachs when it comes to eating processed or packaged foods that often have a lot of sugar and salt. As much as Barney may have enjoyed eating these salty crackers, it did not agree with his canine physiology and the boy should have never left the box where Barney could find it.

Boy: **"Why are you being so stubborn, Barney? Come on! It's just the neighbor's cat hiding behind that bush."**

Barney: *"It smells like a rabbit! Let me go flush it out!"*

Lesson: Sometimes we humans forget that things that seem insignificant to us can be a big deal for a young scent hound, and in this case, Barney was on the scent of what he thought was a rabbit and his urge to chase was making him appear to be stubborn.

Chapter 14: Surprise Bonus Chapter

Dad: "What have you done to my vegetable garden, Barney! You've dug up all my radishes! What's wrong with you?"

Barney: *"Wait a minute - nothing wrong with me! I could smell a mouse was rooting around in the radish patch and I thought I could catch him for you."*

Lesson: Often we tend to quickly blame our canine friends when a mess is created for which there seems to be no explanation. We need to first think beyond simply blaming the dog for unexplained disarray, as there is often a good explanation that exonerates your canine companion from any wrong doing. In this case, Barney was being a scent hound and trying to eliminate a rodent threat.

Mom: "Barney! Why are there teeth marks on the TV remote? That's not a toy, you bad dog!"

Barney: *"I needed something to teethe on cause my gums hurt."*

Lesson: When puppies are teething, this causes them pain and they really need something that's immediately at hand that they can chew on to help them feel better. Don't go blaming your puppy when you're not paying attention and you don't have enough things they're allowed to chew at easy reach for them when their gums are hurting.

Boy: "You bad, bad dog, Barney! You've chewed up my laces!"

Barney: *"You let me play with the laces on your old sneakers. What did I do wrong?"*

Lesson: Think about what you or your children allow your canine friend to play with; giving them old discarded shoes, laces, socks or other articles of clothing, etc., to play with causes confusion in the canine mind when you get mad if they decide to chew something that to a dog looks, tastes and smells the same.

Girl: "Mom! Barney's got dog hair all over my bed!"

Barney: *"You let me sleep in your bed when I was a puppy, so what's changed?"*

Chapter 14: Surprise Bonus Chapter

Lesson: If you'd rather not share your bed with a dog that sheds his or her hair, don't make the mistake of allowing them to sleep with you or your children when they're a cute and cuddly puppy. If you do, it's unfair to blame your canine companion for wanting to continue this habit that you or your children literally taught them.

Dad: "OMG, Barney! Where are all the cheese slices I left here?"

Barney: *"You mean the ones on the coffee table? I thought those were for me."*

Lesson: Some dogs, such as the Beagle, will eat just about anything, and cheese for most dogs is high on their list of favorite human foods. This means that you should be smarter than a dog, and not leave food items anywhere within easy reach. Leaving cheese at nose level is just too much temptation for most dogs.

Moral of the Q&A section

Always DO pay attention to what your dog is trying to tell you, because (in addition to the above), there are so many other lessons we humans can learn from our beloved canine companions. Watching out and learning these lessons, and appropriately acting upon them, will help you to raise a Happy Beagle that will never have to experience unwanted behaviors.

There are so many lessons we humans can learn from our beloved canine companions IF we are paying attention.

Before we close this Chapter, I hope you will enjoy the following true short story about a young and playful male Beagle, named *"Chubbs"* who lived in a townhouse with his young family, that consisted of Mom and Dad and two 7-yr-old twin girls, near an elementary/secondary school that was conveniently only two blocks away. This really touching story was narrated to me by the Mom of the family, a good friend of mine.

Where is Chubbs?

Chapter 14: Surprise Bonus Chapter

One spring afternoon, around 2:00 pm, Chubbs asked to go outside in our back yard, as he often did around this time to relieve himself. He was always very discrete about his bathroom routine and chose the same spot, which was partially hidden behind a low bush that grew against the fence in the back corner of the yard.

I never worried about this routine as he always came back asking to be let in after about 5 minutes, except for this afternoon when 5 minutes came and went, and then 10 minutes before I realized that he had not asked to be let in and I couldn't see him anywhere in the yard.

A sense of panic immediately gripped me as I flew out into the yard yelling for a Chubbs that was nowhere to be seen. How had my dog simply vanished into thin air? I was dumbstruck and immediately called for my husband to come and help me look for him.

We both systematically checked every corner of the yard until we finally discovered that Chubbs' favorite bathroom area behind the bush had been obscuring a weak area in the fence that had over several months been slowly disintegrated by Chubbs' urine stream, and what was now left was a Beagle's sized hole in the fence.

Now panic *really* began to set in as we both ran through the house and out the front door hoping that we'd find Chubbs lounging on the front door mat warming himself in the weak spring sunshine. No such luck, as Chubbs was nowhere to be seen, and as the kids were about to be walking home from school, one of us had to stay home.

My husband decided to jump in our car and slowly cruise the neighborhood while I stayed home nervously pacing, while I waited for the kids to arrive.

Approximately 15 minutes later, I could hear squeals of laughter from the girls as they made their way down the block toward our house. I panicked again as I didn't know how I was going to admit to them that I had lost their beloved dog and I could already imagine the screams of hysteria and flood of tears that would ensue.

The front door burst open and in rushed my girls with Chubbs proudly marching right beside them looking so very pleased with himself.

Chapter 14: Surprise Bonus Chapter

Before I could say anything, both girls hugged and thanked me so profusely for sending Chubbs to pick them up and walk them home from school. Apparently, all their school chums thought this was the coolest ever, and my girls were now considered to be superstars with the most amazing dog!

Not knowing whether I should admit my lax care of their beloved companion, I simply said nothing as I watched the happy threesome bound off to the playroom together. Then, I texted my husband that Chubbs was home safe and sound and not to say anything to the girls until after we had a chance to talk about it between us.

When my husband returned home looking a little haggard, but relieved that all had worked out well, we sat down to talk about what had "really" happened. We agreed that first of all, we were so lucky that nothing happened to Chubbs, while he made his way to the girls' school, and second, the hole in the back fence needed to be plugged up.

Until my husband had an opportunity to go to the hardware store, buy the paint and replacement boards for the fence and then find the time to do the work, which usually meant finding a free weekend, it was now another one of my jobs to keep a very close eye on Chubbs whenever he went out into the yard.

The next morning, before the girls ran out the door to walk to school, they both wanted to know if Chubbs was going to be "picking them up" from school, like he did the previous day. Since we hadn't really talked about it, all I could think to yell after them was: *"Well, I'm not sure, we'll see how the day goes",* as they disappeared out of sight.

The morning quickly became noon and time for Chubbs to go out for a bathroom break, so I followed him out to the yard and over to his favorite bush where he usually emptied his bladder. There was the Beagle-sized hole in the fence that was behind the bush, but Chubbs seemed to have no interest in it whatsoever as he quickly turned around and shuffled back inside the house with me.

Before I knew it, it was now 2:15 pm and the girls would soon be coming home from school. I checked to see that Chubbs was soundly

Chapter 14: Surprise Bonus Chapter

snoring on his favorite couch in the living room, and decided I would get busy and whip up a quick batch of peanut butter chocolate chip cookies for the girls to sample when they got home.

I was just putting the last sheet in the oven to bake when I sensed that something was not quite right. I looked at the kitchen clock, which said it was 2:55 pm and then walked into the living room. Where was the previously snoring Chubbs? Maybe he got too warm and moved to his bed in the kid's room. As I saw he was not there either, a sudden panic gripped me as I realized that even though I had locked the doggy door to the back yard, somehow Chubbs had managed to escape.

Now it was 3:00 pm and the girls would soon be walking home, so I could not head out on the street to search for Chubbs and prayed that he had made his way safely to the school to meet his girls again.

Ten more minutes of nervous waiting, and I heard the laughter and excited screams of the girls as they approached the front door of the house with a happy Chubbs at the lead. As I breathed a sigh of relief and opened the front door for them, the girls each gave me such a hug and thanked me so profusely for sending Chubbs to get them, that all I could do was smile back and tell them that their favorite cookies were cooling in the kitchen.

When my husband came home from work a couple of hours later, I took him aside and told him about what had happened AGAIN. At first, he was upset with me for not watching Chubbs more closely, until I told him that I had been watching him and that I had also made sure that the doggy door was locked. He went to check for himself and saw that the latch was now open so the door could swing freely, and he began to question my diligence again.

I swore that the door had been locked, and while sceptical myself, the only explanation was that somehow Chubbs had learned how to unlock it to let himself out. My husband wasn't buying it, so we glared at each other and then I left to get dinner on the table.

That night before bedtime, I told my husband that tomorrow I was not going to take my eyes off of Chubbs for even a minute, and that I would

Chapter 14: Surprise Bonus Chapter

figure out how he was getting himself out. My husband scoffed a bit and then realized that there wasn't much else we could do.

The next day, after the girls had gone to school and my husband to work, I decided that I would secretly "stalk" my wiley Beagle, to see what was really going on. As usual, he asked to go outside to relieve himself around noon, and I watched from the kitchen as he sniffed about his favorite bush, emptied his bladder and trotted back to the door asking to be let in.

He slept in various locations about the living room for the next several hours and around 2:30 pm I decided that I would make sure the doggy door was locked, and then settle myself in a corner where he couldn't see me, but where I could still see the doggy door.

I quietly sat in my hidden corner, from where I could even hear Chubbs snoring, and besides the snoring, all was quiet, until at precisely 2:50 pm the snoring suddenly stopped and I heard Chubbs jump to the floor. Soon, I saw him stealthily walking across the carpet, while looking toward the kitchen (where I would usually be), as he headed to the locked doggy door. He looked around, and seeing nobody, he used his paw to scratch at the lock on the door until he moved the locking mechanism to the unlocked position, and quickly exited into the back yard.

I quickly jumped out of my hiding place and quietly exited the house from the front door so I could sneak around the fence where his hold was located without him seeing me. Sure enough, out through the hole came Chubbs, still looking right and left to ensure nobody was there before he quickly ran across the street and up onto the sidewalk.

I followed at a discrete distance, while he steadfastly headed down the sidewalk toward the girls' school, and there was no mistaking that this was a dog with a mission in mind because he did not even stop to water a tree or bush or investigate any interesting smells along the way.

Sure enough, he went straight for the gate that led into the girls' school and sat there patiently waiting as various children filed past, some

Chapter 14: Surprise Bonus Chapter

stopping to give Chubbs a quick pat on the head, and as soon as he saw his girls, he stood up and ran straight toward them.

Of course, the girls were ecstatic to see him and immediately dropped down onto their knees to hug and pet him, so I took this opportunity to quickly turn about and run back to the house so they wouldn't see me.

Within minutes of me entering the house and pretending to be busy in the kitchen, I heard the happy threesome coming up the front steps and bursting through the door, with the girls screaming "Thanks for sending Chubbs to pick us up from school, Mom!"

Now what was I going to do? The girls were so happy having Chubbs meet them at school, and Chubbs was obviously single-minded when it came to meeting them, and right on time, too. How did he know precisely what time it was and how long it would take him to walk to the school to be there on time? Nothing short of amazing!

When my husband came home from work that day, again we sat down to talk about what had now become Chubbs' daily trek to meet the girls after school and what we should do about it. Oh yes, and how I was off the hook about latching the doggy door because now we both knew that it was not me to blame, but that Chubbs was smart enough to know how to unlock the door.

Before we could decide what we needed to do about it, the phone rang and it was principal Franklin calling from the girls' school. Apparently, Chubbs' daily visit to meet the girls had become all the school could talk about, and he just wanted to remind us that while dogs were not allowed onto the school grounds, since Chubbs somehow knew this and waited patiently just outside the school gate, he was fine with the girls' 4-legged escort.

My husband and I looked at each other and in that instant decided that Chubbs, the amazing Beagle, had decided he was to be the girls' official escort home from school and there was nothing we could do to change his mind.

That weekend, my husband spent many hours working out in the back yard. While you might think he was plugging that hole in the fence,

Chapter 14: Surprise Bonus Chapter

rather, he had cut a hole in the fence and installed a hinged doggy door with the same type of latch that we thought had kept Chubbs inside doggy door securely closed. So now, he could exit through the hole in the fence when he went to escort the girls home from school, without anyone on the outside realizing there was an opening in the fence.

Next school day, I watched closely to make sure that the change to his escape route had not confused him, and saw that I needn't have worried at all, because it took him about 5 seconds to open the latch and off he went.

The girls were 7 years old when Chubbs started escorting them home from school and he continued his vigilant escort service for the next ten years when the girls graduated from high school.

Incredibly, while Chubbs quietly passed away in his sleep only two months after the girls graduated and no longer needed a school escort, the amazing Chubbs is still fondly remembered and talked about by all the children that went to that school.

Lesson to learn: while we always need to make sure that we keep our fur friends safe, sometimes our dogs are so much smarter than we give them credit for.

Chapter 15: Conclusion and Reviews

*"Some days you're the dog,
some days you're the hydrant."*
— Unknown

This book is written to help anyone thinking of sharing their life with the highly intelligent, versatile and athletic Beagle, to first understand whether or not they truly have the time, energy and lifestyle that would be compatible with raising a healthy and happy dog.

Once it's been decided that the popular Beagle is the right breed to share your life with, the purpose of this book is to help you understand how to properly care for them. This will include socializing, training and providing this dog with adequate physical and mental daily exercise, the best food, and a safe environment, so that this dog can live the longest and most contented life possible.

There are already plenty of books written, and many different trainers and opinions concerning how to correct a dog that may be suffering from any number of behavioral issues.

However, to my knowledge, there are no breed-specific books outlining how most, if not all, Beagle issues are unknowingly created by the

Chapter 15: Conclusion and Reviews

dog's guardian. Therefore, this breed-specific book stands out of all other current publications, because it:

- highlights that almost all problems, both mentally and physically, are a direct result of ignorance or unwillingness on the part of the human guardian to learn what their dog truly needs.
- describes in detail what the human guardian needs to understand and commit to doing on a daily basis in order to match the Beagle's needs, so that they can raise a happy, healthy and well-behaved dog that never has to experience behavioral issues.

There is much knowledge for this breed contained within the pages of this book that has been gained over some 40 years working with dogs. This information will help anyone serious about raising a happy Beagle, so that they can easily implement all the practical tips of this book without having to hire a professional to help them correct any sort of future behavioral problems.

In a nutshell, this book contains all you need to raise a Happy Beagle, that will never have to experience unwanted behaviors.

What Past Clients Have to Say

The following are a few happy reviews from some of my past dog whispering clients, who did the work required to turn their Beagle into a happy and well-behaved companion. I have taught these clients how to apply some of the tips and techniques described in this book (such as how to establish yourself as the pack leader) and they easily managed to get back on track to raising a happy and well-behaved companion.

Thus, rather than taking my word for the effectiveness of the methods contained in this book, perhaps you would prefer to take my clients' word!!

> "Thank you for your report and teaching me to be a pack leader ... this has worked remarkably as Drew and Sammy have responded well beyond my expectations... Drew is very calm and relaxed and our walks are now very enjoyable...

Chapter 15: Conclusion and Reviews

I want you to know that I really appreciate your help... Results have been spectacular and both dogs have evolved into superheroes and have accepted me as their pack leader and respond positively..."
~ Klaus, Drew, Sammy & Max the Cat

"I just wanted to thank you again for our lesson today. You really are amazing with dogs. Tim and I learned so much from you, it's really neat to see the difference it makes in the dogs when you take control..."
~ Morgan, Tim, Grizzly, Bella & Bear

"I was at the point I was ready to give Jake away because I was so concerned about how he reacted every time someone came to the door. It was really embarrassing! Honestly, within three hours of Asia being here, Jake was a different dog. We learned how to become the pack leader and control him..."
~ Sharon, Mike & Jake

"My partner and I and our dog Rollo recently moved to Victoria from up north. Rollo, unused to city life and walking on a leash, was nervous and reactive around other dogs. Asia showed us how we need to behave so he could relax. After just one session the difference was very impressive – walks have become relaxing and enjoyable again – for all of us..."
~ Tim, Mary & Rollo

"Thank you for helping me become the guardian that Ida needs. She was a good dog to start with, now she is an incredible dog. She walks well on lead, stays in my unfenced yard, and comes when called. I am often complimented on what a well-behaved dog I have. Thanks for making it all happen..."
~ Kristiane & Ida

Published by Worldwide Information Publishing 2019

Copyright and Trademarks: This publication is Copyrighted 2019 by Worldwide Information Publishing. All products, publications, software and services mentioned and recommended in this publication are protected by trademarks. In such instance, all trademarks & copyright belong to the respective owners. All rights reserved.

No part of this book may be reproduced or transferred in any form or by any means, graphic, electronic, or mechanical, including photocopying, recording, taping, or by any information storage retrieval system, without the written permission of the authors. Pictures used in this book are either royalty free pictures bought from stock-photo websites or have the source mentioned underneath the picture.

Disclaimer and Legal Notice: This product is not legal or medical advice and should not be interpreted in that manner. You need to do your own due-diligence to determine if the content of this product is right for you. The authors and the affiliates of this product are not liable for any damages or losses associated with the content in this product.

While every attempt has been made to verify the information shared in this publication, neither the author nor the affiliates assume any responsibility for errors, omissions or contrary interpretation of the subject matter herein. Any perceived slights to any specific person(s) or organization(s) are purely unintentional. We have no control over the nature, content and availability of the web sites listed in this book.

The accuracy and completeness of information provided herein and opinions stated herein are not guaranteed or warranted to produce any particular results, and the advice and strategies, contained herein may not be suitable for every individual. The authors shall not be liable for any loss incurred as a consequence of the use and application, directly or indirectly, of any information presented in this work. This publication is designed to provide information in regard to the subject matter covered.

The information included in this book has been compiled to give an overview of the subject and detail some of the symptoms, treatments etc. that are available. It is not intended to give medical advice. For a firm diagnosis of any health condition, and for a treatment plan suitable for you and your dog, you should consult your veterinarian or consultant.

The writers of this book and the publisher are not responsible for any damages or negative consequences following any of the treatments or methods highlighted in this book.

www.ingramcontent.com/pod-product-compliance
Lightning Source LLC
Chambersburg PA
CBHW071502080526
44587CB00014B/2185